THE PRACTICE OF PRAYER

by
GEORGE APPLETON
Chaplain of St Luke's Home, Oxford
Archbishop in Jerusalem 1969–74

MOWBRAYS
LONDON & OXFORD

© George Appleton 1979

ISBN 0 264 66560 0

First published in 1979 by
A. R. Mowbray & Co Ltd
Saint Thomas House
Becket Street, Oxford OX1 1SJ

Typeset by Oxford Publishing Services
Printed in Great Britain by
Fletcher & Son Ltd, Norwich

CONTENTS

FOREWORD

Anyone who presumes to teach others to pray must be one who prays. He must be one who values prayer and sees it as the most important activity of life, the most creative, redemptive and effective thing that he ever engages in — for himself, those whom he loves, those for whom he is concerned, and further still the best and most effective thing he can do for God.

I was very fortunate in my early days as a priest to be introduced to a book which I now see to have been seminal in my training — Arthur W. Robinson's *Personal Life of the Clergy*, in a section of which dealing with prayer he sets out four convictions:

> Prayer is work.
> Prayer is important work.
> Prayer is hard work.
> Prayer is my work.

Paul urges us to pray without ceasing. This advice puzzles many of us, until we suddenly realise that he is telling us that prayer is living life in the presence of God, always conscious of Him, constantly referring everything to Him, rejoicing in his wise and loving will for oneself, for others, for the whole of humanity, becoming more and more aware of the unsearchable wisdom and more than abundant grace for all the happenings, difficulties, opportunities and adventures of life.

It is both heartening and humbling to discover how many people are eager to learn to pray, who hope that they may be helped by a quiet day or weekend and are ready to open their hearts to those whom they have invited to be with them. On such occasions I have found it helpful to ask those participating to look back on the way they have come in this desire for a deeper interior life, their needs, difficulties, misgivings, their experiences or hopes, and perhaps to expose the results of this flash-back to the fellowship of the other seekers. The combined exercise encourages those taking part to stammer out their own inner experience, to be comforted by the experience of others in common need as well as by insights which have proved helpful. It need hardly be said that this look-back is more a confession than a confident witness of any spiritual competence. It is walking humbly with God in the company of others.

This small manual is little more than an exposing of how one man tries to pray, and the writing of it reveals how far that one man still has to go. It is offered, at the request of many friends, in the growing understanding of the warning of St Paul's 'Lest after I have preached to others I myself should be a castaway', lest after talking so much about prayer I should fail to be one who prays. So the student is urged to spend more time in actual praying, whether in words, in thoughts, or in quiet, loving touch with God, than in studying what is written. And both writer and reader will be in St Paul's company again when he says: 'Not that I have already attained . . . but I press on'.

This book comprises forty 'lessons' or meditations, a number reminiscent of Moses at Sinai, of Jesus himself in the Jordan countryside after the experience at his Baptism, and of the first disciples between the great events of the 'Resurrection' and the 'Ascension', with the hope of a further great forty days in preparation for our Pentecost and a global acceptance of the outpouring of the Spirit of God.

Grateful thanks are due to Mrs. Diana Hanmer who not only typed the manuscript but took a deep interest in its subject.

May 1979.

1. WHY PRAY

Most people at some time in their lives have found them-selves wanting to pray. It may be at some crisis, perhaps the discovery that they are suffering from a disease likely to be fatal, or the realisation of the limitations and diminishing powers of body and mind which old age brings. In younger years it may be in setting out on some exciting adventure or the choice of what is to be a life-long work. In middle age it may be a sense of happiness in a worthwhile job or gratitude for the love of family.

Family life may equally have its anxious moments, when sexual attraction and being in love need to deepen into tenderness. Or when a loved one is in trouble through accident, illness, misfortune or even failure and we want him or her to be helped, healed and strengthened.

We ourselves may want similar blessing and help in times of difficulty and weakness, when we do not feel able to cope with the problems and demands of life.

There are choices and decisions that have to be made, when we feel the need for guidance and some assurance that we are doing the right thing.

At some time or other we may think that the motive of prayer is to get from God the things we would like to have, whether material or spiritual, or the things we think we need for the doing of His will. Later we may realise that this is a very immature understanding of prayer, but we should not despise this childlike beginning, for any touch with God is of great value, and God is a generous Father who loves to give good gifts to His children.

As we look at the state of the world and hear of earth-quakes, floods oppression and cruelty, senseless killings, we groan at the suffering involved and at our own help-lessness to affect such happenings, when the only words that will come are 'O God! O God!' expressing both despair and appeal. In the official report of the explosion of the first atomic bomb, it was said that the watching scientists and technicians found themselves praying, as if realising the momentous consequences of what had just taken place.

There may be deeper stirrings which come very close to prayer, moments when we realise there is something in us more than body and mind, dim intuitions of a deep self which we are only beginning to discover and which we want to explore.

This is not the final discovery for we want to know the great original Self from whom our selfhood derives. We want to find God, not from hearsay, but in actual inner experience. We want to know the Creator and the meaning of the universe which He has created and the life which wells up within us.

The ultimate explanation of these inner urges and desires may well be that God has taken the first step. Not only has He created us but He come to us, He speaks to us, and our prayer is our response to Him.

If all this is so, training in prayer is of the utmost importance and we should give to it the attention, study and practice that we are willing to devote to worldly skills and vocations.

But enough talking about prayer — Let us pray:

> Lord, teach me to pray, to want to pray, to delight to pray.
> When I pray, teach me to pray with faith, with hope, with love.
> Let me make prayer my first work, my persistent work, my most important work.
> Work that I do for you, for others, for the whole world.
> Let my prayer be a channel for your love, your grace, your peace for those for whom I pray, and for myself, O dear and blessed Lord.[1]

2. FAITH IN PRAYER

If we are to learn to pray, it is clear that we must value prayer, have faith in it, be ready to practise it, without being over-concerned with inner argument about its efficacy. It is not enough to talk about prayer, we have to engage in it. This applies as much to one who presumes to talk about prayer and urge others to pray, as to those who listen and hope to get a clue or two on how to pray.

Faith in prayer is really faith in the God to whom we pray, and with us Christians it is faith in what He has done in Christ and through Christ, not only in the creative and redemptive moment of time in which He lived among us, but in His continuing presence with us and within us.

The first Christians saw God-with-us, Immanu-el, as the message and meaning of Jesus. St. John, even in the unpromising conditions of exile on Patmos, experienced the Everliving Christ, coming to him and saying 'Look, I am standing at your door, knocking and calling. If you hear me and open your door, I will come in and we will share a meal together'. God takes the initiative. He knocks at every door. He calls, as if to say 'Is anyone at home?'

So prayer is a gesture of faith, faith in a God who wants to get in touch with me, a God who comes, a God who speaks and listens, and a God who is humble and loving enough to wait until I open the door in welcome. Then I can say in a Zaccheus-like spirit 'Today salvation has come to my house'.

At the tomb of Lazarus Jesus expressed his faith in God when he prayed: 'Father, I thank thee that thou hast heard me. I know that hearest me always' (John 11: 41). Even when dead physically, I shall be able to hear Christ's voice, as the little daughter of the President of the synagogue at Capernaum, the widow's son at Nain, Lazarus at Bethany.

One of the oldest collects in our Anglican Prayer Book

speaks of God as more ready to hear than we are to pray, giving more than we desire or deserve. More than we deserve.— I can understand that — but God's generosity exceeds all that I desire! St. Paul realised this when he thought of God giving us His Son and all things with Him (Romans 8:32).

So we need faith in prayer, faith in God to whom we pray, faith in Jesus Christ who came to us from God, who is ever present with God, who taught us to pray, and through whom we pray. When there is faith in prayer like this, then there is also joy in prayer, quiet trust, excited expectation, and deep thankfulness.

An exuberant prayer from a Jewish Hasidic mystic can sum up both faith and joy in God, and our gratitude for the gift of prayer:

> Wherever I go — only Thou! Wherever I stand — only Thou! Just Thou; again Thou! always Thou! Thou, Thou, Thou! When things are good, Thou! When they're bad, Thou! Thou, Thou, Thou![2]

3. THE MEANING OF PRAYER

Prayer is the breath of the soul, as essential as breath to the body. One of the early Bible writers spoke of God breathing into man the breath of life so that he became a living spirit as well as an animated body (Genesis 2:7). This divine breath was not only an initial gift of God's creating activity, but a continuing one to keep him spiritually alive, inwardly healthy, strong and creative. When Jesus made his first disciples aware that physical death had not killed him, he sent them out to the world and breathed on them so that they could receive holy spirit (John 20:22).

We often speak of someone being inspired, literally 'breathed into', and on that first Easter occasion as on all others, it was the life that had come through death that he was sharing with his disciples.

It is through prayer that we come to know God, not only to know about Him, but to know Him personally, in experience. Then when we talk about Him what we say will be authentic, for we have met Him, talked with Him, listened to Him, enjoyed Him. Jesus in the great prayer prayed before he went out to Gethsemane said that God had authorised him to give eternal life to all, and that this life consisted in knowing God — 'This is eternal life to know Thee the only God', and John gratefully added 'And Jesus Christ whom Thou hast sent'. So we get to know God in prayer and in Jesus Christ (John 17:2–3).

People sometimes think that the motive of prayer is to get God to do what we want. Jesus at a most critical moment prayed 'Not my will but thine be done!', not in pained resignation but in glad faith that the Father's will is always good, loving, wise, the most effective thing to be done in the worst of circumstances. A modern writer has said 'Our prayers do not change God's mind, elicit his pity or reverse a sentence . . . they allow God to put into operation (in me and through me) something He has willed all along'.

To know God is to know the source of love, for love, says the New Testament is the most essential characteristic of God. We feel his love, we see it expressed so completely and convincingly in the life and cross of Jesus. We realise that *we* are loved and that leads us to become loving in our turn. 'We love Him because He first loved us'. We become loving through being loved, just as small children learn to love from being loved by their parents. And love is the most important thing in life, it is eternal. 'We know' says St. John, 'that we have passed out of death into life when we love . . . ' (1 John 3:14).

One of our oldest prayers goes back to Pope Gregory who sent Augustine to convert us English:

> O Lord, we beseech thee mercifully to receive the prayers of thy people which call upon thee; and grant that they may both perceive and know what things they ought to do, and also may have grace and power faithfully to fulfil the same; through Jesus Christ our Lord.[3]

So prayer helps us to discover God's will and to receive His grace to help us put it into practice.

Prayer is living in the invisible, the spiritual and the eternal — it is a preparation for life beyond death, it is a first instalment of eternal life, a foretaste of heaven.

Three verses from a hymn express this for us:

> Breathe on me, Breath of God,
> Fill me with life anew,
> That I may love what thou dost love,
> And do what thou wouldst do.
>
> Breathe on me, Breath of God,
> Until my heart is pure,
> Until with thee I will one will,
> To do and to endure.

Breathe on me, Breath of God,
So shall I never die,
But live with thee the perfect life
Of thine eternity.[4]

4. PREPARING FOR PRAYER

It is a very wonderful thing that God should come to us, make himself known to us and speak to us. It is equally wonderful that there is something in us that wants to discover and know him, to be guided and encouraged by Him, and to cooperate with Him in building his kingdom of goodness and love. This makes prayer something more than a duty; it is a privilege and even a necessity. It is the most important thing in life, and therefore needs study, training and loving preparation every time we consciously engage in prayer. We should not regard our regular prayer as something that has to be done, or think that as long as we go through the motions and say the words we have done our duty. We need to spend a proportion of the available time in preparation.

I have found it helpful to begin by relaxing the body so that there is no tension in the limbs and the joints, in the shoulders and the stomach, with the hands almost limp, and with no furrowing of the brow in effort. The peace of the body then communicates its peace to the mind, which must lay aside every anxiety, even our concern for what we plan to do for God. We should lie open before God, as an old English writer says, as the earth lies open to the four seasons of the year.

The next step is to collect our thoughts, which in the early moments of prayer are all over the place, and focus them on God. This can often be helped by fixing our attention on the breathing, the quiet intake and output of breath. This is only an exercise in concentration, and when it has been achieved, we transfer our gathered attention to God himself. One of Israel's poets spoke of the prompting of his innermost self which he accepted as God saying to him 'Seek ye my face', to which he replied 'Thy face, Lord, will I seek' (Psalm 27:8).

In this way we lift up the heart to God, for the heart in

biblical understanding is the centre and core of our being, the deep self of which prayer helps us to become aware, the depth where the Spirit of God incarnates Himself in our personality and where He acts and speaks.

In all this preparation there should be a growing desire for God. Another of Israel's psalmists speaks of having a thirst for God, longing for Him as the hunted deer longs for the refreshment and refuge of a cooling stream (Psalm 42:1). Our Lord promises that all who long for God in this way, hungering and thirsting for Him shall be filled.

Having prepared in this attentive and loving way, we can express our faith and need in thought and words, or remain quiet and still, enjoying our communion with God and quietly alert for anything He may want to say, our whole being open for Him to act within us, to sanctify, make us loving and ready for His will.

The Church has preserved for us a collect which every branch of it puts as preparation for its service of Holy Communion, which needs to be said with a pause after each phrase:

> Almighty God . . . unto whom all hearts are open . . . all desires known . . . and from whom no secrets are hid . . . Cleanse the thoughts of our hearts . . . by the inspiration of thy Holy Spirit . . . that we may perfectly love Thee . . . and worthily magnify thy Holy Name . . . through Christ out Lord.[5]

5. JESUS AT PRAYER

The first disciples of Jesus were fortunate in seeing him often at prayer and sometimes they overheard the prayers which he offered to God. St. Luke tells us that at his baptism Jesus was praying when he experienced the power of the Holy Spirit as convincingly as if a dove had descended from heaven with an inner voice assuring him that he was God's beloved Son, and that the Father approved his decision to leave Nazareth, identify himself with the conscience-stricken people who listened to John the Baptist's fiery preaching, and resolve to become a homeless preacher of God's Kingdom and salvation.

He spent the succeeding forty days in the harsh countryside around the Jordan in prayer and meditation, endeavouring to find out from God how he should exercise his ministry and what methods he should employ for winning the world to God. As a result of this long time of prayer, he rejected certain methods which he recognised as subtle temptations which would not achieve God's will, finally choosing the way of love and sacrifice. From the accounts which could only have come from himself, it is clear that he had the whole world in his heart and longed that the earthly kingdoms of men should become the Kingdom of God.

On the morning after a great day of healing in Capernaum, he was up before dawn, again finding out from God the significance of this power and people's recognition of him as a wonder-worker. As a result he went off on a tour of the villages of Galilee, preaching the advent and meaning of the Kingdom.

After the incident of feeding the crowd, when many wanted him to become the King and liberator of their worldly hopes, he retired alone to the hills to pray about this possible development.

He was in prayer all through the night before he chose

his twelve disciples, the number signifying his hope for the renewal of God's people. In the sermon on the mount, he showed how the Law of the Lord should be written in the heart. This included teaching on prayer: not to be undertaken ostentatiously to acquire a reputation for piety, not to rely on many words and empty phrases, but to be in secret in the chamber of the heart. He then gave them the pattern of prayer, so short and clear, to fundamental in faith, so full of meaning.

Sometimes his prayer was overflowing with praise, as when the seventy returned from the mission on which he had sent them: I thank Thee, Father, Lord of heaven and earth, that Thou hast hidden these things from the wise and understanding and revealed them to babes (Luke 10: 21).

It was while he was praying that the transfiguration took place, when in another night in prayer his inner glory shone through and he was strengthened to go forward in trust and obedience towards the threat of opposition and probable death.

His prayer at the tomb of Lazarus showed his reference of everything to God and his faith in the divine response: Father, I thank Thee that Thou hast heard me. I knew that Thou hearest me always. (John 11:41—42).

In the Upper Room when he warns Peter of the danger of being offended and so denying his Master, he adds: But I have prayed for you that your faith may not fail. The writer of the Epistle to the Hebrews tells us that Christ, our great High Priest, always lives to make intercession for all who draw near to God (7: 25).

Before Jesus and the disciples left the Upper Room to go to Gethsemane, he offered a great prayer for them and for all who through them should become disciples: that they and we may be kept in the knowledge of God, guarded from evil, sanctified in truth, united in love, indwelt with the Father and himself, and filled with his own love and joy (John 17).

A short while later in Gethsemane he undergoes an

agonising temptation to shrink from the cross, with a passionate desire to know that the cross is the Father's will, praying that if it is God's will this bitter cup of suffering might be removed from him, ending with words of triumphant faith: Not my will, but Thine be done! (Luke 22: 39–44).

In the hours on the cross we hear Jesus still praying, first for forgiveness for those who had brought him there, then tremendous words of faith when Psalm 22 seemed to express his spiritual loneliness, his triumphant cry as death drew near and he knew that the task that the Father had laid upon him was completed, and finally in the very moment of death another prayer from the Psalms: Father unto thy hands I commend my spirit.

This rather lengthy study of our Lord at prayer shows us the importance and value that he attached to it. If our professions of discipleship are honest and genuine, we shall give the same importance and value to prayer, so each of us should pray:

Lord, let me be a learner in your school of prayer.

6. 'THROUGH JESUS CHRIST'

Nearly all our prayers end with the words 'through Jesus Christ, our Lord'. That phrase is first of all an expression of gratitude to him. We have come to know God through Jesus Christ. He has led us to God, taken us with him to God. He has taught us all that we know of God, for he has come, as St John says, from the Father's heart to make Him known.

All the faith expressed in each prayer has come to us through Jesus Christ. He has taught us to pray and every prayer is an act of obedience to our Master. We have already studied how Jesus prayed, and every prayer is following his example. Yet many people think that if we add the words 'through Jesus Christ' on to our prayer, God is in honour bound to give us what we have asked for.

Jesus put it in another way in his final teaching to his disciples: 'Whatsoever you shall ask in my name, I will do it', and again, 'If you abide in me and I in you, ask whatever you will, and it shall be done for you'. To pray in Christ's name means to pray as he would have prayed. This attaches a stiff condition to his promise. More even than that, for he urges us 'Remain in me and let me abide in you. Then ask what you will'. So the deepest prayer, the prayer that God loves to answer, is the prayer which Christ himself prays in us.

The essence of our Lord's prayer was and is that God's good, loving and wise will shall be done, always and in every circumstance. Praying in that way is to ask what God has already willed, and we can be sure that God is already working to put this into effect. One of the earliest collections of prayers put together over 1500 years ago put this thought very clearly and concisely: Let thy merciful ears, O Lord, be open to the prayers of thy humble servants, and that they may obtain their petitions make them ask such things as shall please Thee.

15

Yet every prayer, however self-regarding, however far it falls short of the prayers of Christ, is a touch with God, an expression of our dependence on him and our faith in him. Perhaps it is no more than touching the hem of his garment, yet that touch draws power and love from him to meet our need. And every touch with him may be an opportunity for him to teach us to pray more truly, more like the prayer that he would pray to the Father, who always hears, and who is more ready to hear than we are to pray.

Jesus reproved his first disciples because hitherto they had asked nothing in his name. We need to examine our prayers to see if they are the kind of prayers that he would pray, the prayers that he promised God would readily answer, because they refer to things He wants done and which He is already doing.

> O Lord Jesus Christ,
> who art the way, the truth and the life;
> we pray Thee
> suffer us not to stray from Thee, who art the way,
> nor to distrust Thee who art the truth,
> nor to rest in any other thing than Thee,
> who art the life.
> Teach us by Thy Holy Spirit
> what to believe,
> what to do,
> and wherein to take our rest.
> For Thine own Name's sake we ask it.[6]

7. THE LORD'S PRAYER —
PRAYING FOR GOD

The first disciples saw Jesus often in prayer, sometimes through the whole night. They probably also heard from friends who had continued with John the Baptist that he had given them some pattern prayer. So they came to Jesus with the request 'Teach us to pray'. The result was the 'Our Father' with its depth of meaning and its brevity of expression.

The first two words are perhaps the most important — 'Our Father'. If we never get any further, but spend all our prayer time in quiet meditation on them and in making real the relationship they suggest we need have no misgiving. Both words are full of meaning, and though we may be praying alone, we include all our fellow disciples and indeed all our fellow humans, for we all owe our being to God and He wants everyone to have the same dependence and love which Jesus had with Him and use the same address which he did. 'Father — my Father — our Father — Father of our Lord Jesus Christ — Father of all — Prototype of all parenthood — Father, dear Father.

The next phrase is equally important — Our Father in heaven, the sphere of the eternal and the spiritual, of perfection, holiness, blessing and love, not far removed, but present with us, perceptible to the eye of faith, tangible to the touch of love, the spiritual country of which we can all be citizens, the final home of the human spirit.

Then follow three clauses which are prayers on behalf of God, great eternal blessings which God wants — the true knowledge of Him and loving reverence, the deepening and extending of His rule in our hearts and in our world, the knowledge and implementation of His wise, good and loving will.

The first of these three prayers for God is that His Name shall be hallowed, for His Name stands for His nature, all that He is, His reputation. Here we are praying that God may be more truly, more deeply, more intimately known, both as seen in the human life of Jesus Christ and in his incarnation within ourselves. May I reverence and love You, may all do so.

Secondly, we pray that God's Kingdom may come, His rule in the hearts and affairs of men, the completion of His creation. Here we pray that we may love God with all our heart, mind and will, that no lesser loyalties may gain control of us, that God may be King in our hearts, Lord of our lives, and the laws of His Kingdom accepted and obeyed in our personal lives and in all our relationships, and extend all over the world in which we live.

Thirdly, we pray that God's good, loving and wise will may be done. Here we are expressing our faith that what God wants done is always the most loving and effective thing that could be done in every circumstance, however difficult, painful or tragic. God wants for us victory over evil, selfishness, hatred, the banishment of war of every kind, the attainment of abundant life, the triumph of love. Often we see the words 'Thy will be done' sadly engraved on tombstones or hear them spoken in despairing resignation. I don't remember them ever picked out on christening cakes or wedding cakes. In every happening, in every disaster, every failure, every opportunity may His loving will be done.

The final words in the first half of this greatest of all prayers, suggest that in the perfect spiritual and eternal sphere, these three prayers are always intended and practised by angels, prophets, saints and an innumerable crowd of holy, humble, loving people from every age, nation, race and religion. And we pray that true knowledge of God, worship worthy of his great love, faithful following of his will and heartwhole acceptance of his Law may be worked out on earth as fully as they are in the spiritual sphere which we call heaven. It looks as if Jesus implied that we could experience heaven here and now if we lived in the great objectives for which he calls us to pray.

Our closing prayer can only be the prayer we have been thinking about:

> Our Father in heaven
> . . . . .
> Hallowed by thy Name!
> . . . . .
> Thy Kingdom come!
> . . . . .
> Thy Will be done
> . . . . .
> on earth
> . . . . .
> as it is in heaven
> . . . . .
> always
> . . . . .
> O Father in heaven

8. THE LORD'S PRAYER —
PRAYING FOR OURSELVES

In the second part of the Lord's Prayer our Lord asks us to pray for the things we need to fulfil the prayers we have prayed for the great things of God in the first half. We need things for both body and spirit, forgiveness for our sins and shortcomings, our need to be alerted to the forces of evil within and without, and we need divine protection in trial and temptation.

'Give us this day our daily bread' — we are bidden to pray for provision for just the one day, the day ahead, to trust God and not to threaten the peace of today by worrying too soon about tomorrow. Our Lord's teaching about the foolishness and subtle distrust of God implied in anxiety is relevant here. This does not mean that we should not look ahead, but that we should not worry.

In this particular prayer we remember people in hunger, poverty and suffering, and our prayer will be more Christlike and valid if we have done everything in our power to answer our prayer. We also pray in this short trusting prayer, for spiritual food for each day, for its duties, its difficulties, its opportunities and adventures, some of which we know about before we pray, but others which will come unannounced. And returning to the needs of all, we pray for the time to be hastened when everyone shall have sufficient food and all that is necessary for the abundant life that is God's will for all his children.

We go on to pray for forgiveness of the sins and failings of the past which have spoiled our service to God and his other children. There are open crying sins obvious to those who know us, there are secret, whispering sins which God and we ourselves only know, the chronic sins, the selfishness entwined with our nature, our lack of care for others, our falling short of God's will and glory. And because we are all involved in human solidarity there is the need of God's forgiveness for the cruelty of men, the lust of power, greed of gain, pride of race, sin against truth, sin against conscience, sin against love.

Our Lord has attached a condition which needs to be fulfilled if we are to experience God's forgiveness — we must be ready to forgive others. We learn that we only remain within the circle of God's forgiveness if we too forgive others for any wrong they have done to us. If I harbour resentment in an unforgiving spirit, I ought to stop praying to God before praying this clause.

I also need protection for the future, for it is so easy to fall back into temptation through weakness, self-will, pride, the pull-back in the memory of past falls, or acquiescence in the persuasions and rationalising of others, or accepting without examination the prevailing assumptions of the world around us.

We need to be alerted to evil, lest it get any entry into mind, imagination or will, and to be protected and saved from evil which comes to us from outside ourselves or rises from within. We must never let ourselves be overcome by evil, but fight it with goodness, trusting in Him who can make us more than conquerors in every attack, trial and temptation.

Finally we conclude the great prayer by returning to the worship of the opening words, acknowledging that it is only through God's faithful love that we continue to live, only through His strength that we are strong, only through His grace that we are able to grow into loving trusting children of His, and brothers and sisters of Jesus Christ, His beloved Son.

Prayer for today:

> Dear Father
>> food for body and soul for all your children
>> forgiveness of our falling-short of what
>>> we can become by your grace
>> alertness to evil and protection in

spiritual danger and trial
for the Kingdom is yours, and the grace is
    yours, and
may there be glory in our obedience.
    Dear Father!

9. THE JESUS PRAYER

One of the great devotional treasures of the Greek Orthodox Church is what is called the Jesus Prayer. It is short
and simple, so its repetition is easy. It consists of the words

> Lord Jesus Christ, Son of God, have mercy
> on me a sinner.
> There is a depth of meaning contained in
> each word.

Lord — indicating out loyalty, obedience and
devotion to Jesus

Jesus — recalling the simplicity, compassion and
love which we see in the Gospels. We also
remember the meaning of our Lord's
human name — Saviour, the one through
whom God's salvation is made available to
us.

Christ — speaks of the fulfillment of the hopes of
the past and reminds us that he is the One
who was anointed with the Spirit and who
gives us the Spirit.

Son of God —tells us of our Lord's close loving intimacy
with the Father, and the Father's assurance
that he is indeed God's beloved Son in
whom the Father is well pleased.

have mercy — the Greek word *eleison* comes from the same
root as 'olive', and speaks of the soothing,
comforting healing quality of God's mercy,
of which olive oil is a symbol, as well as
mercy in forgiveness.

on me — conscious of myself and my personal need
of comfort, healing, strengthening, mercy
and forgiveness.

a sinner — conscious of my sins and unworthiness
and of how far short I fall of God's holiness

and love, and of how much I need his forgiveness and sanctifying grace.

When we use this method of prayer we don't need to
work out its meaning every time, as I have just tried to
explain it; we assume all that wonderful content of
meaning.

Our Orthodox friends combined the repetition of the
Jesus Prayer with breathing, some taking a deep breath
halfway through: Lord Jesus Christ, Son of God . . . have
mercy on me a sinner. Others do so after each point,
driving the meaning deep down into the heart: Lord . . .
Jesus . . . Christ . . . Son of God . . . have mercy . . . on me . .
. a sinner.

The Orthodox monk or devout lay person, will repeat
the prayer many times, occasionally a thousand times or
more. We in the restless, active, time-controlled West are
not likely to be as dutiful as this, but twenty-five to fifty
times may well be possible, I have found the use of this
prayer very helpful in waking periods of the night. Sometimes I fell asleep still saying the prayer, but console
myself with the thought that I could not fall asleep on a
better occupation.

Our prayer for today must clearly be a praying of the lovely
Jesus Prayer in the way we have been studying.

10. DESIRE FOR GOD

Jesus taught us that the greatest thing in life is to get to know God in personal loving intimacy, to share his life and to have his Spirit living within us. The is the life that never dies and which is deepened and enhanced when we move from the physical and material dimension into the dimension of the spiritual and eternal. It is a quality of life that we can begin to have here and now. If we have God with us and in us He will supply that life. Our hope and desire must therefore be for God Himself.

The Psalmists expressed this faith and desire with deep longing in words which should often form part of our prayers. Psalm 16: 2 prays, 'O my soul, thou hast said unto the Lord: Thou art my God, my goods are nothing unto Thee'. Later translators deepen the meaning: I have no good beyond Thee (RV); My welfare rests on Thee alone (Moffatt). God is to the writer his chiefest good, his highest value.

Psalm 42: 1–2 likens this desire to spiritual thirst: Like as the hart desireth the water-brooks: so longs my soul after Thee, O God. My soul is athirst for God, yea, even for the living God: when shall I come to appear before the presence of God? The writer of Psalm 63 expresses the same longing: O God, Thou art my God: early will I seek Thee. My soul thirsteth for Thee, my flesh also longest after Thee: in a barren and dry land where no water is.

Psalm 72: 24–25 makes it clear that the writer's desire is for God and God alone: Whom have I in heaven but Thee: and there is none upon earth that I desire in comparison of Thee. My flesh and my heart faileth: but God is the strength of my heart and my portion for ever.

If our desire for God is as single and deep as this we shall also long for his good, wise and loving will to be done, and for his rule to govern our desires and actions. We need from time to time to examine our inner life searchingly to

25

see if we do or do not desire God, his will and his Kingdom as the earlier believers of whom we have been thinking, knowing that our desires are known to God and that the thoughts and values of our hearts need cleansing by Him and unifying in Him.

Two earlier teachers and practitioners of prayer have given us supporting insights. St Augustine (4th century) says 'All the life of a good Christian is nought but holy desire'. This insight is quoted by an anonymous English writer 1000 years later who comforts us with 'For not what thou art, nor what thou hast been doth God regard with his merciful eyes; but what thou wouldest be'. For Christians this desire would be to be like Jesus, who enacts before us and in us both the life of God and the life of man.

If our inner being lies open before God, waiting and receptive for his activity within us, we shall find that He puts into our minds good desires and also provides the encouragement and grace to put these holy desires into good effect.

We can be helped by a prayer from a Hindu man of prayer, whose prayers express the warm loving devotion that has always been an element in Indian spirituality. Rabindranath Tagore prays:

> That I want Thee, only Thee — let my heart repeat without end. All desires that distract me, day and night, are false and empty to the core.
>
> As the night keeps hidden in its gloom the petition for light, even thus in the depth of my consciousness rings the cry: 'I want only Thee'.
>
> As the storm still seeks its end in peace when it strikes against peace with all its might, even thus my rebellion strikes against thy love and still its cry is — 'I want Thee, only Thee'.

We Christians can gratefully pray this prayer with him.

11. THE VALUE OF SILENCE

Jesus on at least one occasion warned his disciples not to fall into a common unspiritual mistake of thinking that God will respond more quickly and generously to much speaking 'and long prayers'. He himself loved to go apart into the silence of the hills or the quiet of the night to be alone with God. We cannot imagine him pouring out words, however worshipful or loving, all the time. Often there would have been long periods of silence when he enjoyed being with the Father, who was the great priority and centre of his life. We who have answered his call to be his disciples in our noisy world today will want to learn from his example, his teaching and practice.

We remember, as he must have done, Elijah at Mount Horeb, in the depression that followed his great victory over the false prophets at Mount Carmel. In his days and nights there he experienced a hurricane wind, an earthquake, a desert fire, but the Lord was not in the wind . . . not in the earthquake . . . not in the fire . . . and after the fire a still small voice'. One of the manuscripts has the words 'a sound of gentle stillness' in place of 'a still small voice', and it was in the stillness, without and within, that the prophet heard the voice of God speaking to him.

One of the psalmist-poets, contemplating the revulsions of nature and the upheavals of nations heard a voice within him saying 'Be still then, and know that I am God', an intuition even more relevant as we think of the happenings and sensational headlines of today

There are differing forms of silence. There is the silence of growth, the seed growing secretly, the treasuring of the word after its hearing or conception, nursing the seed until it germinates and takes form.

There is a silence of worship and wonder in the sight of something beautiful, or the realisation of the goodness and the love of God, when thoughts and words have done all they can, an experience leading to a gasp of delight and a quiet trust in the goodness and providence of God.

There is a silence of suffering, when nothing seems possible, except perhaps the acceptance of its mystery and our seeming powerlessness. We think of the Suffering Servant of Isaiah 53, or of Jesus before his accusers and judges.

There is a silence of availability, when we expose ourselves to the Creative Spirit, as Mary of Nazareth did in her response to God 'Behold, the handmaid of the Lord, be it unto me according to Thy word' or Isaiah at the close of the vision in the Temple worship when he cried out to the divine need of a messenger 'Here am I, send me'.

There is a silence of love, as when husband and wife after years of deepening affection, sit by the fireside together in the quiet of the evening, with no need of words.

There is a silence of waiting, of quiet assurance that God will speak within the trusting heart or act in some way which will be recognised as wise, creative and redemptive, as when one of the psalmists says 'For God alone, my soul waits in silence'.

After such a lesson in silence, it would not be disciple-like to end with words, through perhaps we might be gently taken into silence by a verse from a familiar hymn:

> O sabbath rest by Galilee!
> O calm of hills above,
> Where Jesus knelt to share with Thee
> The silence of eternity,
> Interpreted by love!
> Interpreted by love![7]

And now, my soul, let thought and words and love merge into silence.

12. THE PRAYER OF QUIET

If we come from God, belong to God and when we die go
to God, if we believe that God speaks and guides us, if we
believe that it is not only possible but vitally important
that we come to know God in experience, then we must be
ready to learn and practise quietness in prayer.

Meister Eckhart, a German mystic of thirteenth century speaks of this quietness of spirit as the highest form of
activity: When we keep silence and let God work and
speak, simply keeping ourselves receptive, we are more
perfect than when at work.

A modern student of the great people of prayer down
the centuries, Evelyn Underhill, reinforces this: Man's
state of maximum receptivity is when he is abiding
inwardly in simplicity and stillness and utter peace.

Isaiah perceived this many centuries earlier, in a period
of considerable unrest and anxiety: In returning and rest
you shall be saved, in quietness and trust shall be your
strength. (30: 15).

The psalmists experienced this quietness of spirit: I
have calmed and quieted my soul, like a child quieted at
its mother's breast, like a child that is quieted is my soul
(131 RSV).

So we should look at our practice of prayer to ensure
that there is this element of quietness, before we pray,
during our time in communion with God, and as we linger
in his presence almost reluctant to return to the noisy
activity of life. Let us reflect purposively on a further
urging of Evelyn Underhill:

> Give the contemplative faculty its chance, let it
> breathe for at least a few moments each day the
> spiritual atmosphere of faith, hope and love, and the
> spiritual life will at least in some measure be realised
> by it.

And if we want to express this in words, a prayer from Père Grou, a teacher of prayer in France in the latter part of the eighteenth century, can take us into quiet stillness:

> Teach us O God that silent language which says all things. Teach our souls to remain silent in thy presence: that we may adore Thee in the deeps of our being and await all things from thee, whilst asking of Thee nothing but the accomplishment of thy will. Teach us to remain quiet under thine action and produce in our souls that deep and simple prayer which says nothing and expresses everything, which specifies nothing and expresses everything.[8]

13. WAITING ON GOD

Jesus lived so close to God that he seemed to know instinctively when the time was right to act or when he should wait for the signal from the Father. We read in the Gospels of occasions when he said 'My hour is not yet come', followed later by action which showed that the right moment had come. As the Passion came near he saw that his greatest hour had come: 'Father, the hour has come; glorify thy Son that the Son may glorify Thee'. He waited for the word from God, the signal to act and the power to act obediently and rightly.

Preparing his disciples for the time when he would no longer be with them, he told them that they were to wait for the promise of the Father — the coming of 'another Paraclete' who would carry on his own ministry and clothe them with power from on high. The Father's promise was so wonderfully fulfilled in the experience of Pentecost, which was not just one isolated incident, but the beginning of a new era.

The word 'wait' suggests the need to go to God who will show us the meaning of each situation and what He wants us to do. Isaiah at a time of great anxiety in Jerusalem said: In returning and rest you shall be saved; in quietness and in trust shall be your strength. In another text he warns us 'He who believes will not make haste', meaning that those who trust in God will not be impatient, nor act precipitally; they will 'rest in the Lord and wait patiently for Him'. The writer of Psalm 62 shows us an example of waiting upon God: Leave it all quietly to God, my soul, my rescue comes from Him alone. Rock, rescue, refuge, he is all to me, never shall I be overthrown'. (Moffatt's translation).

A later Isaiah, expecting the return to Jerusalem from deportation in Babylon, speaks of the supporting strength of God in the hardships and dangers of the journey: They

31

who wait for the Lord shall renew their strength, they shall mount up with wings like eagles, they shall run and not be weary, they shall walk and not faint. In our journey through life we are promised strength when sudden decisions are needed or emergency strikes us, and when we have to keep going under pressure, and also in the long stretches of unexciting faithfulness and duty — if we wait upon God.

The more we wait upon God, the nearer we come to Him, the more truly and intimately we come to know Him, so much the more we realise our own need of change, our own shortfall of what God means us to be. We begin to understand and want the new birth of which Jesus spoke to Nicodemus. With St Paul we long for the new man to come forth and we wait for the whole man, we pray for this to happen and we realise that it is something given from above — we wait on God to draw us out into this new being, so that Christ may be in us, and we in Christ.

Let these thoughts in our hearts lead us into quiet trusting prayerfulness. If we want to express our trust and thankfulness in words, the following prayer may help:

> Dear Lord, quieten my spirit, and fix my thoughts on thy will, that I may see what Thou wouldest have done, and contemplate its doing without self-consciousness, without inner excitement, without haste and without delay, without fear of other people's judgements or anxiety about success, knowing only that it is thy will, and must therefore be done quietly, faithfully, and lovingly, for in thy will alone is our peace.[9]

14. LET GOD SPEAK

It must be clear that only when there is regular silence within the spirit of man is there hope of hearing God speak. He does not thunder from heaven in a voice audible to everyone, as people at one time seemed to believe. As Elijah discovered, he speaks in a still small voice within the heart.

I have often been asked about the language in which God speaks. Some Jews with whom I have talked assert that He speaks in Hebrew. Muslims insist more strongly that He speaks in Arabic, the language of the Qur'an. Cynical critics in the West suggest that He talks in English, with a growingly American accent. My own belief is that He speaks in the language of the heart. This needs to be interpreted into thought and then expressed in words, and clearly there is both a gap in time as well as in clarity. The great prophets were ready to spend days in waiting upon the Lord and listening for a word from Him.

How can we be sure that something which arises in the mind comes from God? From what we know of God through prophets and saints, through the Bible, and above all from our Lord, we can be sure that it will be righteous and loving, and that it will pierce to the heart of the matter about which we are inquiring and praying. The Jewish-Christian writer of the Letter to the Hebrews gives us this guidance: The word of God is something alive and active; it cuts like any double-edged sword but more finely and it can slip through the place where the soul is divided from the spirit, or joints from the marrow; it can judge the secret emotions and thoughts (4: 12 Jerusalem Bible). There is no secret corner in the heart where the Spirit of God cannot penetrate. So the word which God speaks will cut through all pretence and evasion and go to the heart of the matter in question.

It will also persist, for God never changes, and prayer will not change his mind or will. So if an inner urging keeps returning we should look at it more confidently and hopefully. Circumstances may change, there may be new and hitherto unperceived relevance, but the essential message remains the same.

People in the Bible often received a message from God through dreams, though as with our dreams the meaning was hidden in a little drama, almost like a film, which needed to be interpreted in terms of the circumstances and concerns in which the dreamer is involved. Not all dreams come from God for many are messages from our own subconscious telling us about what is going on in the depths of our own being.

While a word from God may often awaken conscience and arouse a sense of self-judgement, there will be times when it brings comfort, encouragement and assurance about our attitudes, intentions and actions, bringing guidance in perplexity.

The God who reveals Himself in the Bible is a God who speaks, but people must listen. The boy Samuel who helped Eli in the sanctuary at Shiloh was wakened by a voice calling his name and thought it must be Eli calling. Eli, not judged as a very worthy priest or effective prophet, finally perceived that it must have been God wanting to speak to the child and so bade him answer if the voice came again and say 'Speak, Lord, for thy servant heareth'. We need Samuel's childlike spirit and the tired old priest's spiritual perceptiveness to pray Samuel's simple prayer. A verse from the Psalms can also help us to a listening ear, 'I will hearken what the Lord God will say concerning me, for He will speak peace unto his people and to his saints'.

If we really believe that God speaks in the heart of man, we should be eager to listen. A glad prayer from a modern teacher of prayer expresses this for us:

Speak, Lord, for thy servant heareth. My knees are

bowed, mine eyes close, I cover my face, I forget the earth.

O Lord, my heart is ready, my heart is ready; my mind awake, attent, alert; my spirit open and ardent, abandoning all else, holding itself in leash, straining the eye of faith, hearkening for thy step, distant and nearer, leaping with love, throbbing loudly, yet lying still; Speak, Lord, for thy servant heareth.[10]

15. GOD'S PART IN PRAYER

God knows each of us intimately, for we are His creation. He has put something of Himself into us, and it is there that He comes to visit us. He is the One to whom all hearts are open, all desires known, from whom no secrets are hid. We cannot hide from Him, however much we try. He knows us through and through, better than we know ourselves.

He takes the initiative, and it is His action within us that moves us to pray. As one of our oldest Christian prayers says, He is more ready to hear than we to pray. He wants us to enter into a loving relationship to Him. He calls each one of us by name and waits for us to answer. He speaks and hopes that we will listen.

God makes known His will. Often we are called to make choices and decisions. How do we find out what God's will is? Often our choice is clear, and there should be no hesitation in the choice between what is good and what is evil, what is true and what is false, what is loving and what is selfish. Sometimes, however, the choice is between two things which seem equally good, or between two paths neither of which is completely good. How do we discover God's will in such cases?

I find in my own experience that there are certain conditions which have to be fulfilled: (1) Reference to God of all the problems, attitudes, opportunities and decisions of our lives and willingness to receive insights from others, but not allow them to decide for us; (2) Readiness to accept and do God's will without any reservations or conditions; (3) When some intuition comes, to examine it carefully to discover if there is any ulterior self-regarding motive involved; (4) Patient, waiting upon God until a persistent feeling of rightness comes; (5) Quiet putting into practice the guidance received, without dithering or looking back. If we act in faith and in reliance upon God

He can guide us, even if we make an occasional mistake.

The question arises of God's answers to our prayers. Sometimes the answer is yes, sometimes no, occasionally not yet. I have been learning something deeper — that God is his own answer to our prayers. We have called Him in and He is now present in the situation about which we have been praying. He is present with us and our hearts can be at peace.

As we take more and more things to God in prayer, as we commune with Him and grow in personal knowledge of Him, we shall find that we begin to share the mind of Christ. The experience of Isaiah will be ours, almost instinctively and immediately: your ears shall hear a word behind you, saying 'This is the way, walk in it', when you turn to the right hand and to the left. (30: 21).

The Holy Spirit not only speaks, guides and directs, but He acts within the spirit of man. He dwells within man

> to sanctify
> to give courage and grace
> to make us loving.

He gives the sevenfold gift of wisdom, understanding, counsel, spiritual strength, knowledge, true godliness and holy fear.

He helps us to understand the meaning of what is going on in the world, to discern the signs of the times, to diagnose the causes of our unhappy troubles.

We speak of the fellowship of the Holy Spirit. He knits us together in love, urges us towards unity.

He also makes us aware of the ultimate triumph of goodness. The gates of hell shall not prevail against the Church that is strong in the faith of Jesus Christ. Many Christians think of forces of evil besieging the Church, but the invasion force is the Church, storming the gates of hell and releasing the prisoners.

But for all these blessings to operate we must put God first in everything, love Him with all our being. We have to commit ourselves to his cause, not call Him to bless our plans and efforts. For the Creator Spirit will be no man's afterthought. If we seek His help it must be as leader, inspirer, initator of all that is to be done. The creative energy of God must have absolute priority. Then and then only, may we call Him to our aid, and claim His promises.

A prayer of King Henry VI aptly summarises today's meditation:

> O Lord Jesus Christ, who hast created and redeemed me, and hast brought me unto that which now I am, Thou knowest what Thou wouldest do with me; do with me according to Thy will; for Thy tender mercy's sake.[11]

16. VOCAL PRAYER

Most people who pray probably began to pray using almost entirely vocal prayers. Similarly corporate prayer in church services understandably uses mainly vocal prayers, though with a widespread desire for a deeper spiritual life greater use is being made of silence at key points of worship, in intercessions, and often after readings from scripture to allow the passage read to make its own impact and relevance to those who have just listened to it.

No private prayer is well prayed without the pauses and ponderings which call out the powers of mind and heart. Many vocal forms are but mental prayer compressed and uttered in a definite, legible structure for the benefit of the wider family of God. The Lord's Prayer is an example of this, compressed tightly and so concisely expressed that considerable time might well be spent in meditating on each clause and expanding its content. Vocal prayers have often issued from the prayer of quiet in the heart of the writer and can lead back into quiet contemplation within the heart of the reader or the listener.

Many of the ancient collects preserved in the Book of Common Prayer are so short and clear that they are heard too quickly and the mind and the ear has hardly had time to register them before the minister has passed to the next prayer. In structure these collects consist of one sentence only, consisting of five parts: (1) The address to God, expanded (2) by a relative clause indicating the grounds on which we approach Him; (3) the petition; (4) the purpose of our petition; (5) the ending.

This can be seen in one of the most lovely of these ancient collects: (1) O God; (2) who hast prepared for them that love Thee such good things as pass man's understanding; (3) pour into our hearts such love toward Thee; (4) that we, loving Thee above all things, may attain thy promises, which exceed all that we can desire; (5) through Jesus Christ our Lord. We could well spend a minute or two on each of the five parts, allowing the meaning to sink down into the heart.[12]

Sometimes with specially selected prayers or some new prayer I have often felt that I needed to read it or hear it read first of all so as to understand the meaning of what is to be prayed, and then repeat it slowly as a prayer. Unless something like this is done, there is a danger of merely reciting the prayer or listening for its meaning and relevance rather than praying it. Praying alone it is much easier to do something like this.

A litany form enables this to be done, especially if there is a silence after the bidding or petition, followed by a versicle and response.

Today let us pray again the lovely collect set out in this meditation, punctuating it with silences and loving devotion.

17. PRAYING WITH THE BIBLE

The Bible is a library of short books, written over a thousand years, in which people recorded their experience of God, the messages they received from God, the comfort and strength they drew from God. They poured out their hearts to Him, sometimes in suffering and need, even in bitter complaint, but equally in trust, thanksgiving and worship. As they looked back at significant events in their history as a nation they became conscious of God's guiding and blessing hand, and were convinced that God had chosen them to be His priests and prophets to the world, so that all could become God's people, live according to His Law and share in his salvation. The Bible can be a source book for our meditation as well as for our study.

We can select an incident or passage or character and ask ourselves three questions: (1) What was the original context of the selected subject, picturing the scene and seeing what it meant to the people involved? (2) What does it say to us today in our situation, how is it relevant to me? (3) What am I going to do about it, what differences should it make to my thinking, attitudes and behaviour? This is very much a method of the mind and will, but we are commanded to love God with all our mind and will.

Another simple method is directed to our Lord Jesus Christ with warm devotion. After preparation by relaxing body and mind, collecting our attention and lifting the heart of God in desire and love, we read a passage from the gospels slowly and prayerfully in three acts: (1) Jesus before the eyes, looking at him, rather than thinking about him, imaginatively picturing the scene, watching him act, listening to what he is saying; (2) Jesus in the heart, waiting quietly in his presence, so that he may infuse into us the spirit we have seen in the particular incident; (3) Jesus in the hands resolving that we will put into practice

41

what we have seen, heard and felt. These three acts can be summarised as adoration, communion and co-operation.

A less active form of prayer might begin with a word spoken by God or by our Lord. After the same preparation we might repeat the text perhaps twenty times or more, then think it a similar number of times until it penetrates into the depth of our being, and we no longer just think it, but begin to feel it and experience it. Let me give an example which I have found very helpful in a busy life when I have often felt hurried or under pressure: the promise of Jesus to his disciples: 'Peace I leave with you, my peace I give unto you'. As I repeat this text slowly and gratefully, it makes its impression on my mind. As I think it, it goes deep into my being, and I begin to feel the peace of God taking possession of me. This experience of God's peace may last for a few seconds only, or if I hold my mind still it can last for a much longer time. Then as conscious thought returns, I thank God for His peace and resolve that it shall guard my heart and mind for the future.

I can engage in this quiet form of meditation in a similar way, by choosing a text addressed to God by a loving and grateful worshipper: 'Whom have I in heaven but Thee, and there is none upon earth that I desire in comparison of Thee': 'Lord, to whom (else) shall we go, Thou hast the words of eternal life'; 'Show thou me the way that I shall walk in, for I lift up my soul unto Thee'; 'Lord, evermore give us this bread'. The Psalms and the Gospels are full of sayings like these which can lead us into quiet, loving devotion, and the Bible as a whole is an inexhaustible storehouse of the prayers of earlier believers and pray-ers which we can make our own.

> O Holy Spirit of God, help me to hold myself quietly in thy presence, and open my whole being to Thee that Thou mayst dwell within me to speak, sanctify and bless, and fill me with love.[13]

18. THANKSGIVING IN PRAYER

In the Lord's Prayer Jesus taught us to pray for the great eternal things which God wants and which He is always working to bring about — the true and reverent knowledge of Himself, the deepening and extending of His rule in our hearts and in our world, the doing of His wise, good and loving will. We ought to be equally grateful for the great things He has done already.

The Prayer of Thanksgiving in the Prayer Book expresses this in unforgettable words: Almighty God, Father of all mercies, we thine unworthy servants do give Thee most humble and hearty thanks for all thy goodness and loving kindness to us and to all men. We bless Thee for our creation, preservation, and all the blessings of this life; but above all, for thine inestimable love in the redemption of the world by our Lord Jesus Christ; for the means of grace, and for the hope of glory.

Each night before we go to sleep we might make a practice of looking back over the day, and thanking God for all its blessings, for his presence always with us, for the love of family and friends, for every kindness received from others, for new apprehensions of truth and beauty, for the knowledge that we are held safe in his hand whatever happens.

As we look back with grateful hearts, we shall commit ourselves in trusting faith to God for the future, which will be bright with the remembrance of God's goodness in the past. We shall echo the Psalmist's thankfulness and trust: O give thanks unto the Lord, for He is gracious, and His mercy endures for ever.

From time to time it would be good to examine the proportion of thanksgiving to asking in our prayers, remembering our Lord's reproachful remark in the incident of the healing of the ten lepers: Were there not ten cleansed? Where are the nine? Was no one found to return and give praise to God except this foreigner?

As we read the daily papers we and the journalists who report for us tend to take more notice of the tragedies that happen and the evil things that are done than of the good and happy things that are said and done. We must keep our compassionate prayer for those who suffer and sin, but add our thankfulness for those who strive for good, both as individuals and nations.

Above all we need to raise thankful hearts to God for all that He is, not only for all that He has done. The prayer of worship is a more selfless prayer than the prayer of thanksgiving. This is expressed in a prayer that was prayed in Jerusalem around the year 800 AD by a Muslim woman saint, Rabi'ah:

> O my God, if I worship Thee in desire for heaven, exclude me from heaven; if I worship Thee for fear of Hell, burn me in hell. But if I worship Thee for Thyself alone, then withold not from me thy eternal beauty.[14]

19. PENITENCE IN PRAYER

Prayer for forgiveness has always found an important place in prayer, both in the Old Testament and in the New. The nearer we come to God in prayer and the more we come to know Him in personal experience the more we become conscious of the gap between Him and ourselves, his holiness and our unworthiness. We see this realised by Peter in the incident of the great catch of fish on the lake of Galilee, when he suddenly became aware of the goodness and love of Jesus and cried out 'Depart from me for I am a sinful man, O Lord' though this was the last thing he wanted to happen.

Two of the parables of Jesus give us moving examples of penitence and confession. The prodigal son as he sees his father's eager loving welcome cries out from the heart: Father, I have sinned against heaven and before Thee and am no more worthy to be called thy son. And the tax-gatherer who had one day come into the Temple and been moved by the associations of divine holiness and human sinfulness can only whisper, 'God be merciful to me, a sinner'.

Holy people of the past and the occasional holy person in the present whom we speak of as saints, have all been conscious of the need of God's forgiveness. The nearer we come to His holiness, the more we realise our own sinfulness. Penitence will always be part of our prayers, even long after the grateful acceptance of God's forgiveness for actual sins revealed by conscience and growing self-knowledge.

Not only specific sins, single or habitual, need repentance and forgiveness, but a recognition of sinfulness, low spiritual health and sickness. Paul from his contacts with people in different countries around the Mediterranean and from his deep knowledge of both Jew and Gentile, came to the conclusion that all had sinned and fallen short of the glory of God. Failure to live up to God's standards of righteousness and falling short of what we can become by God's grace are equally sinful with specific sinful deeds — failure in trusting faith, failing in truth, love and courage all need penitence and the glad acceptance of God's forgiveness and grace.

The whole sacrificial system of the Old Testament was an expression of the human need and desire for forgiveness, while Christians have seen in the complete obedience of Jesus in life and death the perfect and final sacrifice. As we look at Christ's suffering and death on the cross, with his unfailing love of both God and man, our hearts are moved as deeply as Peter at the lake or Isaiah in the Temple, and we see the cross as God's verification of the forgiveness which Jesus both taught and enacted.

So we pray with the writer of Psalm 51:

> Have mercy upon me, O God, after thy great goodness: according to the multitude of thy mercies do away mine offences.
> Wash me thoroughly from my wickedness: and cleanse me from my sin.
> For I acknowledge my faults: and my sin is ever before me.
>
> . . . . .
>
> Make me a clean heart, O God: and renew a right spirit within me.
>
> . . . . .
>
> The sacrifice of God is a troubled spirit: a broken and contrite heart, O God, shalt thou not despise.[15]

20. FORGIVENESS AND PRAYER

Forgiveness has often been thought of as reconciliation with God, the healing of the relationship which has been broken by our sin. God takes the initiative and in Christ stretches out his hand in friendly love. He says to us 'Child, your sins are forgiven'. They are not regarded by Him as if they did not matter, nor are they condoned. The cross is a measure of the pain that our sins cause to God. It has been said that there was a cross in the heart of God before ever there was one on Calvary.

I must not think that it is my penitence that deserves or wins God's forgiveness; rather, His forgiveness arouses my penitence. God forgives before I repent, but it is my penitence that enables me to avail myself of the divine forgiveness. It inspires in me a deep gratitude, a resolve by His help to sin no more, a desire to set right any hurt or damage that my sin has caused, and a humble and continuing reliance on His grace.

God's forgiveness is unconditional. He will forgive beyond the 'seventy times seven' which Jesus insisted on with Peter. Yet there is a condition which unfulfilled inhibits our acceptance of forgiveness: we must be ready to forgive others any wrongs which we feel they have done to us. God's forgiveness includes us within the circle of his merciful love; if we refuse to forgive in turn we deliberately step outside that circle in which forgiveness operates. With an unforgiving spirit we can say little more than half of the Lord's own prayer; in honesty we have to stop after praying for our daily food. If we fail to forgive we are refusing the friendly relationship with others which we would like God to have with us.

It is a sound practice to include some prayer of penitence, silent or worded, within our evening prayers, when we look back on the past day and become conscious of wrong actions, hurtful words, unloving thoughts, and 'leaving undone those things which we ought to have done'. In this way we allow our Lord to wash our feet and wipe away the dust we inevitably pick up during the day.

The thought of forgiveness deepens our gratitude and love to God. Jesus once spoke of a notorious sinner that her many sins were forgiven because she loved much. With me it is the other way round — because my many sins have been forgiven my heart is warm with gratitude and love, and my time in prayer is a time of restored and joyful touch with God, realised through the teaching, the example and the grace of Jesus Christ.

We can express our thankfulness for God's forgiveness in a prayer that was used by Jeremy Taylor (1613–67), Bishop of Down and Connor:

> Rejoice over me, O God the Father, that this thy child was lost, but is found; was dead, but is alive again.
> Rejoice over me, O God the Son, that thy loud cries and tears and bitter agonies which for my sake thou didst endure upon the cross, were not so unhappily, lost, as to be cast away in vain upon me.
> Rejoice over me, O God the Holy Spirit, that thy so many and powerful touches have at last got the upper hand of me.
> Rejoice over me, O ye holy angels, whose ministry it is to rejoice at the conversion of a sinner.[16]

21. THE PRAYER OF LOVE

Prayer for others, whether loved ones or people in trouble for whom we feel a concern, has always formed a considerable part of Christian prayer. In intercession we act as a link between people in their need and God in his generosity of grace.

Such prayer is an expession of our compassion for people in their suffering, sins and needs, and our compassion grows deeper as we know more of their circumstances, whether as persons or communities. It denotes a growing understanding of the heartache of people, and at the same time a deepening conviction that it is love that saves heartache from becoming heartbreak.

Prayer links the griefs and needs of people with the love and grace of God. We focus the love of God where the need is greatest. Our little human love calls to the infinitely greater love of God to come to the aid of those for whom we are concerned. We lift them up to His presence, hold them in His healing X-ray, His radiant warmth, believing that whatever happens He is with them, all shall be well, nothing can snatch them out of His hand, however far they fall the everlasting arms are beneath.

Distance and time are no difficulty. Our intercessions are like the impulses of electrical energy sent out from a radio transmitter which strike a layer of the atmosphere and are reflected down to the area to which wave-length and direction ae adapted. Our little impulses of love reach the over-arching love and are magnified by the divine energy which makes their transmission possible.

We often say to people when we are in trouble, or they say to us when they are in trouble. 'Well, at any rate you can pray for me', which amounts to thinking of prayer as the last resort when we have tried everything else. If we really believe in prayer it should be the first thing we undertake on their behalf, particularly as people who are seriously ill or troubled find it difficult to pray for themselves.

This demands real faith in prayer, which should move us to prayer as the first thing and the most important thing that we do. Sydney Smith, a canon at St Paul's Cathedral in the first half of the nineteenth century, a popular preacher, a great wit, something of a cynic, but on occasion an honest realist, once wrote in a letter to a friend, 'I am just going to pray for you at St Paul's, but with no lively hope of success'. We all need a more lively hope in God and a deeper faith in the rightness and effectiveness of prayer.

For many years I regarded intercession as a duty, which I did carry out, but with effort and discipline, and it was only when I came to think of it as the prayer of love that it became exciting.

Many of us make lists of people for whom we pray regularly, but it is perilously easy to hurry through our succession of names, whether it be the individual intercessor or the priest in church urging the congregation to pray for the sick and troubled absent ones. I am painfully learning to hold each name in conscious remembrance, repeating the name a number of times in love and faith.

Our expression work for this lesson in our training in prayer could well be to remember lovingly and holdingly those for whom we desire God's will, grace and blessing, offering our love as an additional channel for his.

Praying with love:

> O Thou source of all love,
> let thy love go out to all created beings,
> to those I love and to those who love me,
> to the few I know and to the many I do not know,
> to all of every race,
> to all the living in this world
> and to all the living dead in the next world:
> May all be free from evil and harm,
> may all come to know thy love

and find the happiness
of loving Thee and their fellows.
O let the small love of my heart
go out with thine all-embracing love
for the sake of him who first loved us
and taught us love,
even Jesus Christ, our Lord.[17]

22. PRAYER ABOUT DIFFICULT SITUATIONS

Today our life is so organised and social groupings are so large that the individual sometimes wonders not only about his or her personal value but also about the effectiveness of one person's prayers about the big issues and the difficult situations facing people today.

Our Lord in his own great prayer taught us to pray about honouring God's Name, extending His Kingdom and doing His Will. All co-extensive with humanity and continuing to the end of time.

Tragic things happen, wholesale cruelty takes place, things often seem to have got out of hand, God's hand as well as ours. What can the prayers of one individual or even one congregation do? The first answer to this realistic question is that our prayer keeps such situation tied to God and prevents Him being pushed out.

The second clue is that most man-made situations arise from wrong attitudes within the minds and spirits of people, so that the struggle is basically a spiritual one. Our wrestling, as St Paul reminds us, is not against human foes, but against cosmic powers, against organisations and powers that are spiritual. Now if those powers from the headquarters of evil are able to influence people, surely the powers of good, from the divine headquarters of right and love are able to do the same. Indeed the Bible assures us that they that be with us are more than they that be with them, and if we are for God, as He is for us, who can ultimately stand against us.

If human nature can be infected by evil, surely it is also capable of injections of truth and goodness from their source. The psychologist Jung believed that there is a common unconscious in which we are all included and so able to influence the psychic dimension. Recruit a sufficient number of persuaders, and the whole web of humanity can be charged with spiritual power. The New

Testament also encourages us with the thought that it only needs a small amount of yeast to leaven a whole loaf. Sometimes dreadful happenings leave us speechless in prayer as well as in interpretation; with St Paul we can only groan in dismay and compassion, which the Holy Spirit will turn into prayer intelligible to God. We can only offer our grief and concern and hope to God, with simply a groan and appeal — O God! O God!

Yet as we link these seemingly hopeless situations to God in prayer, He will help us see the hidden possibilities contained within them. And we must never forget that He can influence each of us to right interpretation and thinking, and even to some inspired initiative of love.

Let us remember some of the desperate situations in the world today, express our deep concern to God and our faith that He is constantly at work to remedy them.

23. WORSHIP

The word 'worship' comes from an old English word 'worthship', and so means giving to God his true worth as Creator, Redeemer and indwelling Spirit. It is our response to these divine activities within our spirit and in our perception of God's great loving purpose for the world, to gather all souls in every generation into the embrace of His love. This worship of the heart longs to express itself in words of adoration and praise.

The prophet Isaiah as a young man, present one day in the Temple at the morning sacrifice, saw a vision of the worship of heaven and heard the anthem of adoration of the angels: Holy, holy, holy is the Lord of hosts, the whole earth is full of His glory'. The immediate result of that experience was a conviction of his own unworthiness and need of cleansing and forgiveness. Assured of this by a burning coal from the altar he is ready to offer himself to God as messenger and prophet.

John in lonely exile on the isle of Patmos undergoes a similar experience and hears the adoration of the four great living creatures, representative of the whole creation: Holy, holy, holy, is the Lord God Almighty, who was and is to come'. They are joined by the 24 elders, representing the early and later people of God, by myriads of angels, and by a great multitude from every nation, who in the consciousness of the wonder of creation and redemption, burst into words of worship: Worthy are Thou, our Lord and God, to receive glory and honour and power. And the same ascription of worthiness and glory is addressed to our Lord for his saving work, and for opening to us the books which make clear the loving purposes of God.

The individual response of Isaiah is echoed in each soul that has become conscious of the holiness, glory and saving love of God, and the corporate worship of heaven is re-enacted by the whole Church as it offers the sacrifice of praise and thanksgiving in every Eucharist.

When we worship in this spirit we begin to experience the saving love and power of God. William Temple helps us to understand the consequences of worship in spirit and in truth:

> Worship is the submission of all our nature to God. It is the quickening of conscience by his holiness; the nourishment of mind with his truth; the purifying of the imagination by his beauty; the opening of the heart to his love; the surrender of will to his purpose — and all of this gathered up in adoration, the most selfless emotion of which our nature is capable and therefore the chief remedy of that self-centredness which is our original sin and the source of all actual sin.[18]

When we worship we forget ourselves in the consciousness of the greatness, the holiness, the wonder, the love and the allness of God. On every occasion of prayer there should be some explicit expression of worship. If it comes at the beginning of our time of prayer it will help to make the whole of our prayer more worthy of God.

If we want a form of words to express the worship of our heart we can join in one of the earliest hymns of praise of the Church, the Gloria in Excelsis:

> Glory be to God on high, and in earth peace, good will towards men. We praise Thee, we bless Thee, we worship Thee, we glorify Thee, we give thanks to Thee for thy great glory, O Lord God, heavenly King, God the Father Almighty.[19]

24. SELF-OFFERING

At every Eucharist the Church remembers Christ's offering of himself on the Cross. Words cannot exhaust the meaning or worthily express the wonder of that sacrifice: a full, perfect, and sufficient sacrifice, oblation, and satisfaction for the sins of the whole world.

It was not just an isolated incident but the culmination of a whole life of obedience to the will of God. The writer of the Epistle to the Hebrews suggests that Jesus took as the motive of his life a verse from Psalm 40: Lo, I come to fulfil thy will, O my God, I delight to do it; yea thy law is within my heart. Jesus delighted to discover and to fulfil the Father's will, for he knew that it was perfectly good, loving and wise, the most effective thing that could be done even in the worst of circumstances.

In the Eucharist as we remember our Lord's perfect offering we add our small, imperfect offering to his: And here we offer and present unto Thee, O Lord, ourselves, our souls and bodies, to be a reasonable (*intelligent*), holy and living sacrifice unto Thee. We offer ourselves to God, all that we are, and all that by his grace we can become, in utter simplicity.

The holiness of God embodied and expressed in the life and death of Christ, makes us realise our unworthiness and need of sanctification. We know that the self we offer is an imperfect offering. We cry out with Isaiah 'Woe is me, for my eyes have seen the King, the Lord of hosts!' and with Peter 'Depart from me, for I am a sinful man, O Lord!' But we would be utterly lost if the Lord took us at our word. We offer ourselves to the cleansing fire of the Holy Spirit.

At Passiontide, as we survey the wondrous Cross, we are moved with deep feeling to offer ourselves:

> Were the whole realm of nature mine,
> That were an offering far too small;

Love so amazing, so Divine,
Demands my soul, my life, my all.[20]

Often we sing these tremendous words at the top of our voices; perhaps we should whisper them as we realise what they mean, in the search for God's will in our lives, our willed obedience and the recognition of how much we shall need His help to put them into practice.

I have been greatly helped by the quiet and sober prayer of an anonymous English mystic of the fourteenth century:

That which I am and the way that I am, with all my gifts of nature and of grace, you have given to me, O Lord, and You are all this. I offer it to You, principally to praise You and to help my fellow Christians and myself.[21]

25. PRAYER IN SUFFERING

There is no life in which suffering does not come at some time or other, pain of body, mental illness or anguish of spirit, sometimes so fierce that we find it difficult to pray. Often people say 'What have I done that God should do this to me?' The answer is that God does not cause suffering or inflict it by way of punishment. Yet He is in it, to enable us to bear it and to bring blessing out of it, something greater than if the trouble or pain had never happened.

Paul had a life of considerable hardship, and in addition had some chronic physical ailment which he spoke of as 'a thorn in the flesh'. He prayed that it might be removed, but it was not. Instead he heard within himself God saying to him, 'My grace is sufficient for thee, for my strength is made perfect in weakness', implying that God's grace is available in proportion to the pain and need.

Jesus promised 'Come unto me all that are weary and heavy laden and I will refresh you'. The very remembrance of this can help us, but if we relax and spend time in letting him infuse his strength, we shall be more conscious of that promised strengthening.

People who have come through great suffering and travail tell us that borne with conscious reliance upon God it can bring great blessing, greater than if the misfortune, grief or pain had never happened. They urge us not to let it run to waste.

It is a good thing to pour out one's heart to God, which amounts to sharing the trouble with Him, allowing Him to provide the double yoke and be our partner in it. The poets who wrote the book of Psalms made a practice of this: 'I poured out my complaints before Him: and showed Him of my trouble'; 'when I am in heaviness I will think upon God: when my heart is vexed I will complain'.

One of the great difficulties about severe pain or sickness is that it seems impossible to pray. Here again the psalmist comforts us 'He knows what we are made of, He remembers that we are only human'. Yet perhaps we can shoot up quick darts of love, trusting cries for help, with the faith, however feeble, that He will answer.

Our Lord does not explain the cause or mystery of suffering, He teaches us how to deal with it, assuring us that however much we are knocked about, by His grace we are never knocked out. In all that happens we can be more than conquerors. Nothing can cut us off from his love.

These thoughts are concerned with our own selves in suffering. We also feel the inner urge to pray for those in similar or even more painful circumstances. The following prayer was prayed by Sue Ryder and her husband Leopard Cheshire when after the war they visited the liberated concentration camps in Germany, Poland and Czechoslovakia:

> Grant peace and eternal rest to all the departed, but especially to the millions known and unknown who died as prisoners in many lands, victims of the hatred and cruelty of man. May the example of their suffering and courage draw us closer to Thee through Thine own agony and passion, and thus strengthen us in our desire to serve Thee in the sick, the unwanted and the dying wherever we may find them. Give us the grace so to spend ourselves for those who are still alive, that we may prove most truly that we have not forgotten those who died.[22]

This prayer still needs to be prayed as we think of the killings and brutal deeds still taking place, and a prayer that the promise heard by John in his visions in Patmos may be speedily fulfilled: And God shall wipe away all tears from their eyes; and there shall be no more death, neither sorrow, nor crying, neither shall there to be any more pain. Blessed be God!

26. PRAYER IN BITTERNESS

People who recite the Psalms in an orderly way, working through the whole Psalter every month, will often be troubled, as I am, by verses in which the writers curse their enemies and invoke God's judgement upon them. For years now I have omitted these verses of bitterness as not being appropriate in trying to express the heart's devotion to God.

More recently I have found these uncharitable verses of value, not for devotion, but for psychological self-knowledge. The writers were very human and frank, and I find myself from time to time having to deal with feelings of injustice and bitterness of which I am ashamed and keep out of my prayers, sometimes from a sense of self-righteousness more than one of penitence.

The religious poets of Biblical Israel were not inhibited this way; they poured out their hearts to God and made no attempt to hide their bitterness and their desire for revenge on their enemies — and even their resentment against God. This can be seen in the book of Job, a dramatic poem dealing with what seems clearly undeserved suffering. Job's wife is more vehement and less trusting when she presses him 'Curse God and die!'

To pour out one's bitterness to God is like lancing a boil and observing the spiritual pus which is evacuated. It is safer to do this with God than with a human companion, for He already knows the most secret thoughts and feelings of the hurt heart, and He can sterilise the pus and heal the painful cut.

Jesus on the cross experienced an hour of spiritual loneliness and blackness of spirit in the grip of which the whole world seemed darkened. In that moment of desolation a verse from the Psalms expressed what he was feeling and became a prayer of his own 'My God! My God! why hast Thou forsaken me?' A feeling of forsakeness, but still 'My God!', so an expression of faith at a moment when faith was all that was left. The heart needs to be open to God and its bitterness expressed. If there is only a flicker of faith, God comes to our rescue and our cure. The very act of opening up to Him is an expression of faith.

A New Testament writer warns his readers not to allow any root of bitterness to spring up and affect their spiritual life. If we are at the receiving end of another's bitterness we should not retaliate with bitterness but with compassion, for bitterness is like a cancer in the soul and damages the embittered one more than the one on whom it is poured out. Forgiveingness is the radical cure and those who are conscious of having been forgiven much by God will want to follow the Father's example and live in the spirit of His family.

A prayer:

> O God, You know me better than I know myself; You see all my hidden feelings which I only begin to see when I am habitually in your company. O Holy, Compassionate and Loving One, seek the ground of my heart and examine my thoughts. Reveal to me any roots of bitterness, and lead me into your compassionate forgiving, loving way. I pray this prayer through him who was so uniquely your Son and the embodiment of your nature, Jesus Christ, my Lord.[23]

27. PRAYER IN DEPRESSION

Moods of depression come to almost everyone at some time or other. The usual prescription for dealing with them is a course of tranquilisers. But these do not really deal with root cause. One of the psalmists subject to depression asks himself 'Why art thou so heavy, O my soul, why art thou so disquieted within me?' This is a good question to ask oneself when these dark moods descend on one, and attempting to answer it may reveal reasons for the depression: things did not go as well as I had hoped; I failed in some effort or action; I felt overlooked or lonely; or as I grow older I experience the diminishing powers of body and mind and in retirement perhaps grudge no longer being at the centre of things. To discover a cause is halfway of dealing with it. The psalmist advises us how to deal with it: Put thy trust in God, for I will yet praise Him who is the help of my countenance and my God.' A Jewish writer says that 'countenance' means that which is the representative characteristic of the entire person, meaning our whole attitude and outlook.

Depressing loneliness can be dealt with by recollecting the presence of God and calling to our aid His unfailing grace. Depression calls for a real exercise of faith. It has been said 'That man is perfect who can come to God in the utter dearth of his feelings, without a glow or an aspiration, with the weight of low thoughts, failures and wandering forgetfulness, and say to Him, "Thou art my refuge" '.

Jesus experienced an hour of spiritual darkness and depression on the cross, when a verse of Psalm 22 seemed to sum up his feeling of dereliction: My God! My God! Why hast Thou forsaken me? We often focus our attention on the second part of this verse, but it is the first part that reveals his unshaken faith — in it all, in spite of it all, still 'My God'.

Other psalms bring light and comfort. The best loved of all psalms, Psalm 23, shows us how to pray: 'Yea, though I walk through the valley of deep darkness, I fear no evil for Thou art with me' — even when I enter what sometimes seems the darkest valley of all, that of death.

Psalm 40: 1–3, tells us of the experience of one who had this faith and trust: I waited patiently for the Lord: and He inclined to me and heard my calling. He brought me out of the horrible pit, out of the mire and clay, and set my feet upon the rock, and ordered my goings. After a serious illness or a bout of depression this can be our prayer of thankfulness also.

Depression can be like a dark cloud descending on one. An aeroplane on a rainy day rises through dark clouds to the brightness of the sun, and as we look down on the clouds beneath, they are seen as bright rather than as dark and gloomy, in unending horizons of bright sunshine.

Another exercise of faith in depression is to shoot up little darts of love to God, which pierce the dark overhanging cloud and make a channel of faith through which His infinitely greater love can come to our rescue.

A young Jew wrote on the wall of the Warsaw ghetto:

I believe in the sun, even if it does not shine,
I believe in love, even if I do not feel it
I believe in God, even if I do not see Him.[24]

Such faith can liberate us from any ghetto of depression.

There is further comfort in recognising that in prayer we come nearer to God, and the more we love the world the more keenly we shall feel its tragedies, confusions and massive sins. We shall look through God's eyes and feel something of the pain in His heart, but we shall also see His will to forgive and redeem, and feel his love, grace and blessing at work. And we shall understand more deeply how Christ bore on his heart the sins of the world and brought to us the divine forgiveness.

So at the end of this prayerful exploration into the meaning and cause of depression we lift loving and grateful hearts to God, and with every thought and memory repeat with another psalmist: O give thanks unto the Lord, for He is gracious: and his mercy endures for ever. Let this verse be the theme as in quiet trust we lift our hearts. We can repeat it in words and in thought, until we feel its truth as well as think it.

28. PRAYING ABOUT THE FUTURE

Many of us tend to think about the future with anxiety rather than as an adventure which God will inspire, guide and bless. We worry lest we should fall victim to some disease, lest we should lose some loved one, lest we should lose our money. We worry about growing old with its failing powers, we try to evade thinking about the inevitability of death.

Jesus taught us that worry is not only foolish, but in a deeply subtle way sinful also, for it amounts to distrust of God. In his own pattern prayer he included 'Give us *this day* our daily bread', spiritually as well as materially. We are to live for each day, not letting a feared tomorrow disturb our trust in today. He did not tell us to have no concern for the future, but not to worry about it, rather to trust God for his supporting love in whatever may happen.

There are few lives to which suffering does not come, physical or spiritual. Jesus never explains to us the mystery of suffering but he teaches us how to deal with it. Not in bitterness, nor in defeat, nor in feverish activity to leave no time to remember it, but in acceptance of it as an opportunity for God's grace. As Paul saw in an adventurous life, which had some unexplained physical weakness in it, nothing can separate us from God's love, in everything that happens we can not only get away with it by the skin of our teeth, but be victorious in it. Suffering need not be waste, if our spiritual eyes are open to His presence. Yea, though I walk through the valley of deep darkness, I will fear no evil, for Thou art with me.

Old age can be one such valley, but if we are conscious of the presence of God, the Eternal, the most Ancient of Days, we shall put our hand in His, and go forward trustingly and expectantly applying words at the most famous of all weddings, to each stage of life 'Thou hast kept the good wine until now'.

The darkest valley of all in human thinking is the valley of death. Faith bids us think of it as a birth — into the spiritual and eternal, not going away from home but going home. To the New Testament writers it was as easy as falling asleep here and waking up there. Both Testaments of our Bible assert 'Eye has not seen, nor ear heard, neither have entered in the heart of man the things which God has prepared for them that love Him' and He longs for the love of all.

The Nicene Creed ends with words of triumphant faith 'And I look for the resurrection of the dead and the life of the world to come'.

Praying ahead:

> Grant, O Lord,
> that the years that are left
> may be the holiest,
> the most loving,
> the most mature.
> I thank you for the past and especially that you have kept the good wine until now.
> Help me to accept diminishing powers as the opportunity to prepare my soul for the full and free life to come in the state prepared by your Son, Jesus Christ, our Lord.[25]

29. PRAYING FOR THE DEAD

Jesus spoke of the Father as the God not of the dead but of the living, with specific mention of Him as the God of Abraham, Isaac and Jacob, implying that they were still living. In his parable about Lazarus and the rich man he makes clear his own belief in life after death, in the continuance of memory, in judgement about the past, but with a hint of possible growth in that Dives was anxious that his brethren should be warned and so saved from the spiritual anguish that he was undergoing.

Jesus spoke of the Father's house as having many rooms and said that when he went to the Father he would be preparing a place for his disciples. He promised one of the thieves crucified with him that they would be together after death. His own death and resurrection and the promise of his continuing presence with his followers emboldens us to speak of him as a Go-between-Lord, and to believe with Paul that he is Lord of both the living and those whom we speak of as 'dead'.

If we have offered loving prayers for people with us in this world we shall want to continue to pray for them when they are living but out of our sight in the next world. We pray as we formerly did that God's loving and wise will may be done in them and for them, that they may grow in holiness and love and join the spirits of just men made perfect. I find it helpful and exciting to pray for a growing list of loved ones and friends who have gone over the horizon of our sight into the new dimension of living, during the silence of the Eucharist when I have made my communion with the Risen Lord.

A former canon of St Paul's Cathedral, a great scholar and preacher, suggested that we may still have personal contact with our beloved dead. One who has died speaks to the dear ones who are left:

Death is nothing at all — I have only slipped away into the next room. I am I and you are you. Whatever we were to each other that we are still. Call me by my old familiar name: speak to me in the easy way you always used. Put no difference into your tone, wear no forced air of solemnity or sorrow. Laugh as we always laughed at the jokes we enjoyed together.

Play, smile, think of me, pray for me. Let my name be the household word it always was. Let it be spoken without effort, without the ghost of a shadow in it. Life means all that it ever meant. It is the same as it ever was: there is absolutely unbroken continuity. What is this death but a negligible accident? Why should I be out of your mind, because I am out of your sight?

I am but waiting for you, for an interval, somewhere very near, just round the corner. All is well. Nothing is lost. One brief moment and all will be as it was before.[26]

Many people in tribal religions in different parts of the world believe that they can enjoy contact with their ancestors, while the Chinese people value this continuing truth. The Egyptians have their Book of the Dead and so do the people of Tibet. Hindus and Buddhists believe in a whole series of lives as people advance to the perfection and peace of Nirvana. They will rejoice in the Gospel confirmation of their faith.

Let me close this meditation of prayer with two prayers that I often use:

O Father of all, we pray to Thee for those whom we love, but see no longer. Grant them thy peace; let light perpetual shine upon them; and in thy loving wisdom and almighty power work in them the good purpose of thy perfect will; through Jesus Christ our Lord.[27]

We give back to you O God, those whom you gave to us. You did not lose them when you gave them to us, and we do not lose them by their return to you. Your dear Son has taught us that life is eternal and love cannot die. So death is only an horizon, and an horizon is only the limit of our sight. Open our eyes to see more clearly, and draw us closer to you that we may know that we are nearer to our loved ones, who are with you. You have told us that you are preparing a place for us: prepare us also for that happy place, that where you are we may also be always, O dear Lord of life and death.[28]

30. PRAYER FOR BUSY PEOPLE

Some people live such busy and tiring lives that they have little time or energy left for prayer. Mothers of families often have to get their husbands off to work and their children to school, tidy the house and perhaps do a full or part-time job, and then return to cook the evening meal, retiring tired out at a later hour to bed. How can they be helped to a deeper spiritual life?

Most busy people will be helped by the example of Brother Lawrence, a man of lowly birth, born in 1621, who served as a soldier, later worked as a footman in a wealthy family, and finally became a lay brother in a Carmelite community in Paris. There he was sent to wash the dishes and later to do the cooking in the monastery kitchen until he died in 1691. He wrote a series of letters about the way in which he practised the presence of God.

In these letters and in conversations with a wise priest he explained his practice. His prayer was nothing but a continuous sense of the presence of God. He thought of God as always with him, often as in him. He kept himself in an habitual silent and secret conversation with God. He did even the smallest thing for the love of God. He did not pay overmuch attention to methods and forms of prayer, but simply gave himself to God saying 'Let Him do what He pleases with me', and praying 'Lord, make me according to your heart'. He finally reached a condition in which his times of prayer were no different to other times, for he was always conscious of God's presence with him.

If ever housewives get together to choose a patron saint, Brother Lawrence would be the obvious choice.

Another practice which I have found helpful in a busy life as a diocesan bishop was when pressed or hurried or tired to claim the promise in our Lord's words 'Come unto me all that labour and are heavy laden, and I will refresh you', taking two or three minutes off, relaxing in a comfortable chair, and opening my whole being to his renewing strength.

A prayer which Bishop John Taylor shared with his people when he was installed as their bishop in Winchester Cathedral can inspire and strengthen us:

> Lord Jesus Christ
> alive and at large in the world
> help me to follow and find you there today
> in the places where I work
> meet people
> spend money
> and make plans.
> Take me as a disciple of your kingdom
> to see through your eyes
> and hear the questions you are asking
> to welcome all with your trust and truth,
> and to change the things that contradict God's love
> by the power of your cross
> and the freedom of your Spirit.[29]

The first thing that can be said is that we shall not be judged by the amount of time we spend in prayer, for in the spiritual dimension time does not dominate as it does in the physical. Our desire to pray, our longing for a closer life with God, is a more important criterion.

A second thought is that a quiet touch with God, short though it may be, can bring us to a peaceful heart, if it is unhurried and if we can give our whole attention to God during the few minutes we make available. That quick unhurried touch with God can give us the right tempo for the day, save us from impatience and rush, and in the end actually save time.

31. PRAYING FOR THE CHURCH

Before Jesus left the upper room on the night before he died he prayed a prayer for his disciples and for all who through them should come to faith and discipleship. In this prayer recorded for us in John 17 he prays: Keep them in thy Name; guard them from the evil one; sanctify them in thy truth; may they all be one; may they, Father, be in us, and we in them; may they be with me where I am and see my glory; may they have my joy and may thy love be in them. We can pray this prayer with our Lord for ourselves as individuals and for all members of the Church.

The Church is the Body of Christ, founded to be the corporate representative of him and to carry on his loving, serving, saving work. It is to be the Christ Community, the Community of love. We pray that it may indeed be so.

Christ is the Lord of the Church, and we can be assured that he is always at work in it and on it. He will be urging and directing it towards unity, the unity of his will, attained in the way that he will show us.

The Church is to be holy, with his own holiness, in all its members and in all its branches. If it were truly holy it would soon come to unity, so perhaps we should pray more for its holiness.

The Church is to be Catholic, in fulness of truth and in universality. Our loyalty to Christ and our membership in his Body rises above all differences of race, colour, nation, class and economic status, even above the difference of sex.

It is to be apostolic, conscious of commitment to the mission which he laid upon it, moving out in loving concern for the spreading of his Kingdom and the welfare of all, and for ever preaching his good news of love and calling all into the embrace of the Father's love.

We sometimes think of the Church as a beleaguered fortress beseiged by the forces of evil, whereas it is really

God's liberation army storming the gates of hell and releasing the prisoners of sin and despair.

Churches and congregations always seem to be appealing for money, urging people to support them rather than assuring people that they will be supported in their needs, tragedies and sins.

There is always the temptation to rely on organisation, structures, money raising, and to seek for popular approval, rather than warning people of the consequences of wrong attitudes.

The Church is meant to be the pattern of the world's life, as Christ is the model for the life of the Church. All these thoughts seem to be a litany for the Church, with the versicle and response:

> O Lord of the Church
> Make us the Church of the Lord.

In addition to these petitions we can pray a collect set for Good Friday:

> Almighty and everlasting God, by whose Spirit the whole body of the church is governed and sanctified: Receive our prayers, which we offer before Thee for all members of thy holy church, that every member in his vocation and ministry may truly and godly serve Thee; through our Lord and Saviour Jesus Christ.[30]

32. QUESTIONS ABOUT PRAYER

People nowadays often ask if it is any good praying if they are not sure that God exists. Living in a science-orientated age they would like a scientific proof or logically convincing argument. This is not possible, not yet at any rate, for God is Spirit and so cannot be fully understood, described objectively or grasped by the mind. Science deals with things that can be observed, examined, measured, classified and verified. Faith in God and prayer to Him operate in the spiritual sphere or dimension.

Yet some answer to the question must be attempted. The questioner might be helped by quiet relaxation, by stilling the mind, by becoming open and receptive, not just one single effort of a minute or two, but in disciplined practice. Jesus promised that those who seek shall find. This suggests that God will take the initiative. He will come. He will knock on our door as we knock on His. The Bible presents the faith that God is the first mover, that He acts, speaks, loves and saves.

Much will depend on our hope that there is a God, or our desire for Him, on our readiness to live our lives on the basis of faith in Him, and to put Him as the central reality and chief value in our lives, if we can begin to be conscious of Him.

A second question that arises repeatedly is[6], Is it my good praying when I don't feel like it?' This may best be answered by a parable that was given me over fifty years ago when I was the parish priest in a large group of villages in the Irrawaddy Delta in Burma. A senior woman missionary and I were visiting a riverside village. We arrived there towards sunset, visited the homes of Christians, tried to help a number of sick, and later in the evening gathered in the bamboo school room which also served as a church. We squatted on the bamboo floor round a hurricane lamp. My companion gave a short talk which dealt with this very question. Imagine, she said, a son who has gone to live in a village upstream. Every Sunday he gets out his canoe and paddles down to visit his ageing parents. One week, however, he feels out of sorts, he has a touch of malaria. He says to himself, 'I won't go this week, they won't miss me'. A little later he feels that his mother might fear that he was ill. So he gets into his canoe and is only an hour or so behind his usual time. Imagine, continued my friend, the parents talking together after his return. 'You know, our son was under the weather this week, it looks like malaria coming on. But how good of him to come all the same. What a good loving son he is! How fortunate we are to have him!' The speaker concluded by saying that God is like that. He is so pleased when we pray when prayer is difficult, when the heart doesn't seem to be in it.

When the heart is warm and when the memory of God's goodness in the past wakens loving gratitude, it is easy to pray. When, on the other hand, the heart seems cold and it is difficult to pray, that surely is a worthier offering, which will convince God that we really love Him, that our wills are his, even if our emotions vary.

Other people have asked about the relationship between the more discursive form of meditation and the quieter, more receptive form which we call contemplation. I cannot do better than quote Father Stanton, a well-known and saintly priest who for almost the whole of his ministry was a curate at St. Alban's, Holborn. 'Meditation,' he said, 'is a detachment from the things of the world, in order to attend to the things of God. Contemplation is a detachment from the things of God in order to attend to God Himself.'

Others ask about the use of other people's prayers. I find these helpful as long as they lead me into prayers of my own, whether voiced or silent. They help to push our little boat off from the bank into the main stream, when it gets carried on by the current almost without effort.

We need not worry overmuch about putting our prayer

75

into words or even about using words at all. We need not pay too much attention to methods of prayer, as long as we pray. The great thing is to desire God, to be conscious of His presence, to feel His love — and to enjoy Him.

O God,
I seek to know you in prayer,
to have the joy of knowing that you are.
I know that I cannot
 objectify you,
 describe you,
 reduce you to propositions,
 but only understand by faith.
Reveal yourself to me, I pray, through the records of Jesus Christ and through his everliving presence within me.[31]

33. SOME EFFECTS OF PRAYER

In prayer we come to know God intimately and personally, lovingly and trustingly, and this, as Jesus said in the night of his greatest need is eternal life, 'super-life', divine life. We not only know about God but we know Him in a way that is like the loving intercourse of husband and wife, parent and child, friend and friend, which brings peace of heart and a deep quiet joy. God takes the initiative, He knocks at my secret door, He makes Himself known at unexpected moments, and I learn that He is always present if my spiritual eyes are open to perceive Him.

When I am in communion with Him, a new dimension of time takes over, the tempo of eternity. We live under the pressure of time these days, especially those who work in big cities, but also mothers of families. At moments of pressure it is good to take a few minutes, and let His peace calm us. Time will then seem to slow down, things will line up for orderly attention, in a queue rather than in frontal array. If the heart is unhurried through this touch with God, we shall find that there is plenty of time. Jesus was never hurried, worried or on the edge of a breakdown. We too can live in the tempo of eternity rather than in the pressure of time. If we keep close to God, if only to touch the hem of his garment, we shall find our strength renewed.

Today we like to approach things from the human end, the horizontal and existential. So we examine ourselves experientially, we probe the situations confronting us empirically, practically, concretely. We study man as a phenomenon and religion as a process and observe the effects and consequence.

This is being done about contemplative prayer. Doctors, psychologists and laboratory technicians examine the effect on output of brain energy, breath rate, heart beat and blood pressure. They have discovered that:

oxygen consumption decreases by up to 20% after three minutes quiet meditation, a result that takes five hours of sleep to achieve
the rate of heart beat decreases
breathing rate slows down
with continuous discipline blood pressure becomes slower
the blood lactate which is associated with anxiety decreases.

All this may seem very humanistic and empirical, utilitarian even, yet authenticating the spiritual element of our personality and driving us back to God, the Source, the Power at work within life, the Love at the heart of things.

We hear much about psychosomatic sickness, the interlocking effect of body, mind and spirit. The most obvious example is the occurence of duodenal ulcers in people who worry. Some people who suffer from asthma are weighed down with the burden of life, which expresses itself in breathlessness. Psychologists tell us that migraine is often caused by a fear of ridicule which makes the sufferer want to get away to be alone in the dark. Pains in the body for which no physical cause is discoverable may be due to a desire to escape from the responsibilities of life. Competing claims within the psyche which we cannot or will not resolve may lead to schizophrenia; compulsive stealing may be due to a devalued self or possibly a lack of challenge and adventure in life.

Sickness of heart brought about by spiritual causes can only be cured by spiritual means. Life integrated in God, guarded in peace by our trust in Him, refreshed and renewed by our touch with Him, sense of guilt set right by the acceptance of God's forgiveness can all help towards the abundant life which is His will for everyone.

A prayer to lead us into quiet communion:

O Spirit of God, set at rest the crowded, hurrying anxious thoughts within our minds and hearts. Let the peace and quiet of thy presence take possession of us. Help us to rest, to relax, to become open and receptive to Thee. Thou dost know our inmost spirits, the hidden unconscious life within us, the forgotten memories of hurts and fears, the frustrated desires, the unresolved tensions and dilemmas. Clease and sweeten the springs of our being, that freedom, life and love may flow into both our conscious and hidden life. Lord, we lie open before Thee, waiting for thy peace, thy healing, and thy word.[32]

34. FURTHER CONSEQUENCES

As we get to know God more intimately in a practice of quiet trusting prayer in which our minds are stilled for loving openness to Him, we shall become aware of the gap between His holiness and our sinfulness. This is dismaying at first, and were that all, we should despair. But God whispers within, 'Child, your sins are forgiven'. He takes over if we allow Him to do so, and shows us what by His grace we can become.

The nearer we come to God the more deeply we feel the sins and tragedies of the world, and his compassion floods our hearts. We feel the truth of one of our Lenten hymns:

> There is no place where earth's sorrows
> Are more felt than up in heaven
> There is no place where earth's failings
> Have such kindly judgment given.[33]

This compassion helps to free us from censoriousness, yet without lösing our sense of the damage that sin does to God's children.

As in prayer we keep close to God-in-Christ and Christ-with-God, we shall gradually acquire the mind of Christ, his outlook and attitudes. With Christ's mind we shall almost instinctively and spontaneously see what he wants done and do it in his way. We shall share the experience promised to the prophet Isaiah: Your ears shall hear a word behind you, saying, 'This is the way — walk in it,' when you turn to the right or when you turn to the left.

There is a further effect of prayer which we ourselves may not notice and perhaps ought not to notice, though others may do so, and we may see in others. This is a growing transfiguration which comes from an inner transformation. When Moses came down from Mount Sinai after his forty days in seeking the divine Law by which God's people should live, the waiting Israelites saw that his face was shining with the reflected glory of God's presence, though Moses, said by the Bible to be the most humble of men, was not conscious of this. St Luke tells us that it was while Jesus was praying that he was transfigured before his three watching disciples. St Paul adds that 'we all with unveiled face, beholding the glory of the Lord, are being changed into this likeness from one degree of glory to another'.

Loving communion with God prepares us for the sphere of the eternal and the spiritual, a foretaste of the life beyond. We begin to experience eternal life, resurrection life, here and now. Our true citizenship will be already in heaven.

William of Thierry, a contemplative and mystic who lived from 1085 to 1148 has left us this fatherland prayer which we can make our own:

> Lord, I am a countryman, coming from my country to yours. Teach me
>> the laws of your country
>> its ways of life
>> its spirit
> So that I may feel at home there.[34]

To feel at home with God is perhaps the deepest, loveliest, most desirable gift, made possible because God makes His home with us.

35. DISCOVERING THE DEEP SELF

We have been learning that prayer is a quiet, alert activity within the spirit of the one praying, prior to and more than a form of words spoken by the voice. We lie open before God in all moods, circumstances and happenings as the earth lies open to all weathers. I have found that this kind of prayer somehow illuminates the interior life and helps me to discover my real self. It may even be thought of as an exploration into inner space, which finally discovers the very springs of being from which my life flows and where the Spirit of God operates.

Dag Hammarsjöld, the former Secretary-General of the United Nations, describes this exploration in a devotional diary which was only discovered after his tragic death:

> The longest journey
> Is the journey inwards.
> Of him who has chosen his destiny,
> Who has started upon his quest
> For the source of his being.[35]

St John of the Cross again helps us from his own practice and experience of prayer:

> The centre of the soul is God, and when the soul has attained to him according to the whole capacity of its being, and according to the force of its operation, it will have reached the last and deep centre of the soul, which will be when with all its powers it loves and understands and enjoys God.[36]

St Augustine urges us on in this journey of discovery:

> Seek for yourself, O man; search your true self. He who seeks shall find — but, marvel and joy, he will not find himself, he will find God, or, if he find himself? he will find himself in God.[37]

We are beginning to anticipate what St Paul longed for 'when that which is perfect is come . . . then shall I know even as I am known'.

The discovery of this inner self, the very core of our being, where we are created in the image of God, where the Holy Spirit speaks and acts, needs to be offered to God at every stage. A prayer already quoted by an anonymous English writer of the fourteenth century helps us to do this:

> That which I am, the way that I am, with all my gifts of nature and grace, you have given to me, O Lord, and you are all this. I offer it to you, principally to praise you and to help my fellow Christians and myself.[38]

And a psalmist reminds us of the Holy Spirit's knowledge of our spirits, as well as our need of honest self-knowledge and our need of sanctification:

> O Lord, thou hast searched me out, and known me: thou knowest my down-sitting, and mine up-rising; thou understandest my thoughts long before.
> Thou art about my path, and about my bed: and spiest out all my ways.
>
> . . . . . .
>
> Try me, O God, and seek the ground of my heart: prove me, and examine my thoughts.
> Look well if there be any ways of wickedness in me: and lead me in the way everlasting.[39]

Our prayerful study today can conclude with a prayer prayed by a member of the Society of Jesus in Japan:

> O Christ my Lord, I pray that you will turn my heart to you in the depths of being, where with the noise of creatures silenced and the clamour of bothersome thoughts stilled, I shall stay with you, where I find you always present and where I love and worship you.[40]

36. PRAYER AND THE ETERNAL PURPOSE

The opening verses of the Bible picture the Spirit of God brooding over the original lifeless, shapeless, unordered matter as if seeing its final order, wonder and beauty. Geologists tell us that the universe is much older than men thought it to be, an age of 1000 million years, compared with the six thousand years since man began to record his history and consciously order his religious life. God is the Eternal. As a psalmist says: a thousand years in thy sight are but as yesterday.

The Bible opens with words of faith: In the beginning — God. It goes on to speak of men's experience of God, of words which men heard spoken in the depths of the heart, sometimes only dimly perceived, but often clearly and simply worded with the ring of truth which they felt compelled to obey. Early men felt a presence in nature, a mystery which they could not grasp, but which moved them to wonder and to something akin to prayer and worship, sometimes to fear.

The people of the 'First Covenant' saw God working in their history, revealing his nature, his eternal plan, sending messengers and prophets to rebuke, guide and encourage them, to be the people of God and to bring a blessing to all nations, with a gospel that all were called to be people of God. They began to see that God was not only righteous but loving, that his Spirit was being poured out on people everywhere.

Christians saw the climax of love in Jesus, with God's nature and will expressed in a human life, culminating in unfailing obedience in death and continuing in unkillable life and spiritual presence, so that all could be rescued from failure and sin and united with God in and through him.

Today we are learning more of the experience of people of other faith and religion, interpreted in terms of their own history, culture and spiritual genius, using different names for the transcendence to which they give their worship and loyalty and the immanence they perceive as present and active. It is exciting to learn of the experience and faith of others, and to share with them our own.

As we look at the universe in which we live we marvel at its mystery, its wonder and beauty, its order and coherence, its ever expanding potentiality for the life of man, we feel that we can never exhaust our benedicite: O all ye works of the Lord, bless ye the Lord, praise Him and magnify Him for ever!

Nor can we fail to add our wonder at the life of man which the Creator Spirit has brought to its present stage — discovery and achievement, technological skill and efficiency, art, music and peotry, human love, compassion, desire that all should have the abundant life of the Creator's will. Truly, it seems to many, man is made in the image of God.

Yet there is also the black shadow of suffering, cruelty, widespread hunger and disease, war, premature death. Men often hold God responsible and pray that He will put things right, yet most of these dismaying flaws can be set right by human endeavour and commitment. It is in the spirit of man that things have gone wrong: if people ignore or starve the spiritual constituent of personality implanted by God, they will be frustrated, selfish, destructive and unhappy. If we refuse or fail to live together as the children of God and the family of mankind, things will continue as we see them at present. We must be creators of our human society, helping the Creator to complete the creation on which He has been at work through countless aeons.

St Paul thought of Christ as progressively overcoming evil until finally he will offer the completed kingdom back to God, and God will be all in all. God wills to gather all humanity, in every generation into the embrace of his eternal love. St John in the final book of the Bible, looks into the world of the spiritual, where the kingdoms of the world are becoming the Kingdom of our God and of his Christ, when there will be no more suffering and pain, when God will wipe away every tear in his completed and perfected creation.

In the beginning — God, at work throughout time — God, in the end — God. Blessed be God! Let me lift up my wondering, longing soul to God, in silent worship for all that He eternally wills to do. 'Thy Will be done, Thy Kingdom come, on earth as it is in heaven!'[41]

37. ANSWER TO PRAYER

God Himself is the answer to all prayer. We have called Him in to our situation with all his goodness, love and wisdom. If He is present with us we need have no fear or anxiety. He will guide, his grace will be more than sufficient, his gifts will progressively operate within us. His Spirit in us will give understanding in the meaning of things, wisdom to know what ought to be done; guidance so that we can be creative and helpful; spiritual strength to stand firm in all doubt, difficulty and despair; knowledge to understand all the factors involved; godliness to be his child and to have his mind and character; and holy fear which is the loving reverence of a child who fears lest he should fail the Father, eagerness to understand and obey.

Jesus said 'Whatsoever you should ask the Father in my name He will do it'. A stiff condition is attached, for 'in my name' does not mean just tacking on 'through Jesus Christ' at the end of every prayer, but praying as he would pray, asking only for the things that he would ask.

John remembered Jesus putting it in another way: If you abide in me and I in you, ask what you will and it shall be done unto you. This is, if anything, an even stiffer condition. It amounts to allowing him to pray in us, in our name. These two interlocking conditions suggest that Jesus Christ is the answer to all our needs and longings.

There needs to be a believing persistence in prayer. Jesus told two parables to illustrate this: the first of an unjust judge who would only answer the importunate plea of a widow who had been wronged, not because of the justice of her case but to rid himself of her persistent importunity; the second of a man in sudden need at night, who would keep his neighbour from sleep and awaken his family until his urgent needs were met. This does not mean that we should badger God to answer our prayer, but that if unjust judges and unwilling neighbours will in the end yield to such pressure, then God who is so loving and generous will be more ready to give than we to ask. The greatest gift that we can ask for is His Spirit.

Sometimes our faith and trust are tested by delayed answers to even Christlike prayers. A Methodist lay preacher and I were once talking about John Wesley's experience in the Aldersgate meeting house when his heart was strangely warmed and he knew that Christ had saved him. The preacher asked me if I knew how long John Wesley had prayed for this to happen, and when I confessed my ignorance he replied 'Over ten years!' When the prayer was answered, it was infinitely greater than he knew, more even than he had prayed for.

Jesus in the hour of agony in Gethsemane prayed that God would take away the cup from him, and added, not in resignation to an arbitrary and omnipotent God, but in glad acceptance of the wise and loving Father 'Nevertheless not what I will but what Thou wilt'. 'Thy will be done' is always the wisest, most trusting, most loving prayer in every circumstance. It has been said that our prayers 'do not change God's mind, elicit his pity or reverse a sentence . . . they allow God to put into operation (in me and through me) something He has willed all along'.

There is a further condition before we can expect God to answer even our most compassionate and urgent prayers. This is that before asking Him to act we should have done everything in our power to answer our own prayers. We pray most earnestly that God will give peace in the world, and that He will feed the hungry millions. He wills both of these, but if we spend 20 times as much money on armaments as we do on helping poor nations to feed their hungry people, we are shuffling off our responsibility on to Him.

A prayer which has been prayed by the Church for over 1500 years sums up our search for the ways in which God answers prayer:

> Almighty and everlasting God, who are always more
> ready to hear than we to pray, and art wont to give

more than either we desire, or deserve: Pour down upon us the abundance of thy mercy; forgiving us those things whereof our conscience is afraid, and giving us those good things which we are not worthy to ask, but through the merits and mediation of Jesus Christ, thy Son, our Lord.[42]

38. DISCIPLINE IN PRAYER

Jesus once told his first disciples that people engaged in worldly work were often wiser than those who claimed to be childen of light. They are ready to undergo training, undertake their duties faithfully and punctually, study new ways and examine their practice and progress. Prayer is of such importance that we should be ready for training and discipline. Study of this small manual can provide training, and the discipline will come afterwards. Prayer can help us in this life, providing insight, guidance and grace, and can prepare us for life in the world to come, the sphere of the spiritual, rather than the physical and material.

It is good that people should have a rule, however simple. The temptation at the start is to be too idealistic and heroic with the probability that it may have to be scaled down later and so involve a sense of failure. It is better to begin with something simple and practicable; it can always be stepped up later in the light of experience and a desire to know God more personally and deeply.

For most people early morning and late evening before retiring to sleep seem to be the best time for prayer, but some people have to leave home early and travel long distances to their work. Even a short time of prayer would keep us in touch with God, for example it takes barely a minute to say the Lord's Prayer slowly and thoughtfully, and this can begin the day with God. Travelling to work can offer the opportunity for moments of meditation and quick arrow prayers, while even reading the newspaper can suggest thanksgiving for good things that advance the Kingdom or sorrow for the disasters that happen and the crime perpetrated.

But any time is right and good, and any touch with God brings grace and the assurance of His love. Any place too can reveal His presence. It is good to have a quiet place available, but this is not always easy, but it is always possible to withdraw into the chamber of the heart and shut out every thought but that of God. Our churches might be more used, and when I was a parish priest in the City of London some thirty or more people would drop in for a few minutes on their way to or from office or in the lunch hour.

We would like to spend enough time in prayer to express our devotion, but with disciplined training we shall not be uneasily conscious of time, with one eye on the clock. In the spiritual dimension length or shortness of time do not seem to operate, only the desire of the will and the love of the heart.

With an inner reverence posture does not matter greatly — kneeling, standing, sitting or lying in bed or walking the heart can be lifted to God or God can make Himself present to us.

It would be good to have a regular time of intercession when we offer the prayer of love for those whom we love and those in need of God's comfort and love. This could form a part of our evening prayer, with perhaps a longer period once a week. I make a habit of praying for the departed during the quiet moments when other people are making their communion.

There should be a quiet preparing of body and mind before every time of prayer, and training in attention, so that every time the attention wanders or is distracted by some movement or noise we can firmly but gently bring it back to God. This small manual of training has emphasised the importance of silence, when the voice is silent and the mind is still, with the whole being open and receptive, so that He can speak or work within us with his sanctifying grace.

It may be possible to have at least once a week a longer period of meditation, when an incident or passage from the Bible can lead us into communion with God. This can be done either alone or in company with a group of like-minded people.

We will need to ensure that the main constituents of prayer should find a place — worship of God for what He is, thanksgiving for what He has done, loving prayer for others and for His Kingdom, with penitence for remembered sins and for the ways in which we fall short of His will for us, what we can become by His grace.

More important than all these clues to prayer is the confidence that the Lord who taught his first disciples to pray in Palestine will also be with us today and train us wherever we may be or wherever we may go and whatever may happen.

We can pray again and regularly the prayer we used at the first lesson of this plan of training:

> Lord, teach me to pray, to want to pray, to delight to pray.
>
> When I pray, teach me to pray with faith, with hope, with love.
>
> Let me make prayer my first work, my persistent work, my most important work.
>
> Work that I do for you, for others for the whole world.
>
> Let my prayer be a channel for your love, your grace, your peace for those for whom I pray, and for myself, O dear and blessed Lord. [43]

39. ALWAYS SEEKING

In a short, clear, amazingly comprehensive verse in the Sermon on the Mount, Jesus says: 'Ask, and it will be given you; seek and you will find; knock and it shall be opened to you.' This verse is generally interpreted as referring to three aspects of prayer. The seeking of which our Lord speaks is primarily a search for God, a desire to know Him personally and intimately, a knowledge which confers on us eternal life, the deepest and highest kind of life, the deathless quality of God's own life.

St Paul in his great poem on love says that our present knowledge is only partial, hazy, blurred, but when the complete and perfect is come, we shall see face to face, and know as fully as God knows us.

In setting out the blessedness of the Kingdom, Jesus includes the beatitude of the pure in heart, the single-hearted who seek God, put Him as the supreme value in life, whom we love with all our being, and promises that we shall see God. It was said of Moses that God used to speak to him face to face as a man speaks to his friend.

God has given us great help in this seeking and finding in the life of Jesus and in the indwelling of his Spirit within our hearts: God has shined in our hearts to give the light of the knowledge of the glory of God in the face of Jesus Christ.

It has been said that we could not seek God unless He had already found us. Our seeking is in response to His finding.

One of the psalmists expresses his longing in the words 'When shall I come and behold the face of God?' Another prays: 'Hear, O Lord, when I cry aloud, be gracious unto me and answer me.' When Thou hast said, 'Seek ye my face', my heart says to Thee, 'Thy face, Lord, do I seek'.

God is always present throughout his creation, his Spirit fills the universe, there is no place where He is not present. When He asks, as Jesus did of blind Bartimaeus, 'What do you want me to do for you?', I reply with him, 'Master, let me receive my sight', so that my spiritual eyes may be opened, and I see Him who is invisible, except to the eyes of faith and love.

To pray today:

> O Christ,
> I used to think I had
> to keep seeking,
> to keep asking,
> to keep knocking
> until you responded.
> Now I know that I have
> only to seek and I shall find,
> only to ask and you will answer,
> only to knock and your door will at once be opened.
> You do not demand importunity but simply faith,
> O gracious, self-giving Lord.[44]

40. PRAYER: SPIRITUAL HUNGER: PENTECOST

We sometimes get depressed as we look at the state of human society — the wars, materialism, class selfishness, violence, abandonment of ethical standards, confusion in a period of rapid change. Many are equally worried about the poverty and ineffectiveness of the Churches and religions, and the great increase in psychological and spiritual sickness. It looks as if the diagnosis of the prophet Amos is as valid in our generation as it was in the ninth century BC: 'A famine . . . not a famine of bread, nor a thirst for water, but of hearing the words of the Lord'. There is a widespread spiritual hunger.

There is growing awareness of this spiritual famine. The great psychologists have made us aware of the inner and deeper life within ourselves. Psychiatrists help people to track down and recognise the causes of our psychological disease and sickness. Everywhere — in almost every country and among people of other religions as well as our own, there is an interest in prayer and a desire for a deeper spiritual life.

The Maharishi and his training in what he calls 'Transcendental Meditation' — TM for short — has attracted many thousands of people, particularly young people, who have been willing to pay a substantial fee and undergo a strenuous course of training. There are classes for people engaged in financial business who find such training beneficial in that it helps them to be calm, quiet and alert, and so able to make more money. Young officers in training at Westpoint, USA, undertake such training, and find that it equips them to be quicker and steadier in military efficiency. But the true TM specialists want their students to find God.

Buddhist monks in Western countries have founded monasteries to train people in the highest stages of concentration and contemplation, helping people to a deep stillness of mind that opens the way to Nirvana, the state of enlightenment, the perfection of being and blessing.

Sufis, originating within Islam, have become almost ecumenical in teaching their way of meditation and prayer.

Teachers of Zen, originating from Buddhism, are training people to quiet stillness, so that they break through the cerebral barrier into direct contact with reality. They are making us aware that there is something beyond intellectual activity and discursive meditation.

Hindu swamis attract many people who desire the contemplative life and a release from illusion, vanity and sin. There is also within Hinduism a strain of warm, loving devotion, known as 'bhakti', going back to the Gita, which was such a source of inspiration to Mahatma Gandhi. We can find this warm loving devotion expressed in the poems and prayers of Tagore.

Muslims show their faithfulness to the five times of prayer each day and to see a Muslim spread out his prayer mat at the appointed times, wherever he may be, is an example of discipline in prayer, even if it sometimes becomes formal, as all forms sometimes do.

In the Christian Church people eagerly welcome training in prayer given by teachers who pray as well as talk about prayer. When people in our Churches learn of the rich heritage of prayer preserved for us and begin to practise quiet contemplative meditation which leads to communion with God, they ask 'Why have we not been taught this before?'

More and more clergy are realising that they are not primarily social workers, efficient organisers, experts in raising money, but humble, loving practitioners of prayer, and trainers in spirituality, consultable by their people who recognise the need for a deeper spiritual life. Many of us also are concerned that the public prayers need to be prayed and not just recited, perhaps with little pauses after each clause of prayer.

We are also realising what spiritual treasures we have in our religious communities whose members have devoted the whole of their lives to worship and prayer, and hope that we can receive vocational training in courses varying from single quiet days perhaps to several months.

The eye of faith can see in all this hunger for a deeper spiritual life and the evidence of world-wide interest and readiness to be trained, the activity of God, who meets every human situation with the appropriate and contemporary spiritual initiative and remedy.

There is in it all a vision of spiritual revival longed for by the prophet Joel when the Spirit will be poured out on the whole of humanity, young and old, men and women, without distinction of class; experienced by the twelve apostles at Pentecost, by people in spiritual movements all down the centuries, by people today who long for the deeper spiritual gifts. There is a call to go into training, each person for his or her own sake, for the sake of true religion, for the sake of the world, for God's sake, to prepare for God's next Pentecost.

O God, we pray for Thy Church which is set today amid the perplexities of a changing order, and is face to face with new tasks: fill us afresh with the Spirit of Pentecost; help us to bear witness boldly to the coming of Thy Kingdom; and hasten the time when the knowledge of Thyself shall fill the earth as the waters cover the sea.[45]

SOURCES

1   Dean Eric Milner-White *My God My Glory* (SPCK)
2   Jewish Hasidic Devotion
3   Book of Common Prayer (BCP). Sacramentary of Pope Gregory c.600 AD
4   E. Hatch, Hymns Ancient and Modern Revised 236
5   BCP Sacramentary of Pope Gregory
6   Erasmus 1466–1536
7   J.G. Whittier A & M Revised 184
8   Père Grou SJ 1731–1803
9   G.A. *One Man's Prayers* (SPCK 1967)
10   E. Milner-White *My God My Glory* (SPCK)
11   King Henry VI
12   BCP Sacramentary of Pope Gelasius c. 500 AD
13   G.A.
14   Rabi'ah c. 800 AD
15   BCP Psalm 51:
16   Jeremy Taylor (1613–67) *Jubilee of a Penitent Soul*
17   see (9)
18   William Temple *Readings in St John's Gospel*
19   BCP
20   Isaac Watts A & M (R)
21   The author of *The Cloud of Unknowing* in *The Epistle of Privy Counsel*
22   Quoted in Mary Cragg *Blessings*
23   G.A.
24   Quoted in Hans Kung *On Being a Christian* (Collins)
25   see (9)
26   Henry Scott Holland Canon of St Paul's Cathedral 1884–1910
27   1928 Prayer Book
28   Source so far untraced, slightly adapted.
29   Bishop John Taylor
30   BCP (slightly adapted) Sacramentary of Pope Gelasius c. 500 AD

31 G.A.
32 G.A. *Jerusalem Prayers* (SPCK)
33 F.W. Faber 1814–63 A & M (R) 364
34 William of Thierry (1085–1148)
35 Dag Hammarsjöld *Markings*
36 St John of the Cross 1542–91
37 St Augustine of Hippo 354–430
38 *see* (21)
39 BCP Psalm 139
40 Quoted by Father Enomiya-Lasalle SJ in a book on Zen Meditation
41 G.A.
42 BCP (slightly adapted) Partly Leonine Sacramentary and partly Gelasian
43 *see* (1)
44 *see* (32)
45 Source so far untraced